Practical Java™

Programming Language Guide

Addison-Wesley Professional Computing Series

Brian W. Kernighan, Consulting Editor

Ken Arnold/John Peyton, *A C User's Guide to ANSI C*

Matthew H. Austern, *Generic Programming and the STL: Using and Extending the C++ Standard Template Library*

David R. Butenhof, *Programming with POSIX® Threads*

Brent Callaghan, *NFS Illustrated*

Tom Cargill, *C++ Programming Style*

William R. Cheswick/Steven M. Bellovin, *Firewalls and Internet Security: Repelling the Wily Hacker*

David A. Curry, *UNIX® System Security: A Guide for Users and System Administrators*

Erich Gamma/Richard Helm/Ralph Johnson/John Vlissides, *Design Patterns: Elements of Reusable Object-Oriented Software*

Erich Gamma/Richard Helm/Ralph Johnson/John Vlissides, *Design Patterns CD: Elements of Reusable Object-Oriented Software*

Peter Haggar, *Practical Java™ Programming Language Guide*

David R. Hanson, *C Interfaces and Implementations: Techniques for Creating Reusable Software*

Mark Harrison/Michael McLennan, *Effective Tcl/Tk Programming: Writing Better Programs with Tcl and Tk*

Michi Henning/Steve Vinoski, *Advanced CORBA® Programming with C++*

Brian W. Kernighan and Rob Pike, *The Practice of Programming*

S. Keshav, *An Engineering Approach to Computer Networking: ATM Networks, the Internet, and the Telephone Network*

John Lakos, *Large-Scale C++ Software Design*

Scott Meyers, *Effective C++ CD: 85 Specific Ways to Improve Your Programs and Designs*

Scott Meyers, *Effective C++, Second Edition: 50 Specific Ways to Improve Your Programs and Designs*

Scott Meyers, *More Effective C++: 35 New Ways to Improve Your Programs and Designs*

Robert B. Murray, *C++ Strategies and Tactics*

David R. Musser/Atul Saini, *STL Tutorial and Reference Guide: C++ Programming with the Standard Template Library*

John K. Ousterhout, *Tcl and the Tk Toolkit*

Craig Partridge, *Gigabit Networking*

J. Stephen Pendergrast Jr., *Desktop KornShell Graphical Programming*

Radia Perlman, *Interconnections, Second Edition: Bridges, Routers, Switches, and Internetworking Protocols*

David M. Piscitello/A. Lyman Chapin, *Open Systems Networking: TCP/IP and OSI*

Stephen A. Rago, *UNIX® System V Network Programming*

Curt Schimmel, *UNIX® Systems for Modern Architectures: Symmetric Multiprocessing and Caching for Kernel Programmers*

W. Richard Stevens, *Advanced Programming in the UNIX® Environment*

W. Richard Stevens, *TCP/IP Illustrated, Volume 1: The Protocols*

W. Richard Stevens, *TCP/IP Illustrated, Volume 3: TCP for Transactions, HTTP, NNTP, and the UNIX® Domain Protocols*

Gary R. Wright/W. Richard Stevens, *TCP/IP Illustrated, Volume 2: The Implementation*

Please see our web site (http://www.awl.com/cseng/series/professionalcomputing) for more information on these titles.

Practical Java™

Programming Language Guide

Peter Haggar

ADDISON-WESLEY

An imprint of Addison Wesley Longman, Inc.

Reading, Massachusetts • Harlow, England • Menlo Park, California
Berkeley, California • Don Mills, Ontario • Sydney
Bonn • Amsterdam • Tokyo • Mexico City

Many of the designations used by manufacturers and sellers to distinguish their products are claimed as trademarks. Where those designations appear in this book and Addison-Wesley was aware of a trademark claim, the designations have been printed in initial caps or all caps.

The authors and publishers have taken care in the preparation of this book, but make no expressed or implied warranty of any kind and assume no responsibility for errors or omissions. No liability is assumed for incidental or consequential damages in connection with or arising out of the use of the information or programs contained herein.

The publisher offers discounts on this book when ordered in quantity for special sales. For more information, please contact:

Corporate, Government, and Special Sales Group
Addison Wesley Longman, Inc.
One Jacob Way
Reading, Massachusetts 01867

Visit AW on the Web: www.awl.com/cseng/

Library of Congress Cataloging-in-Publication Data

Haggar, Peter, 1965-
    Practical java programming language guide / Peter Haggar.
        p.   cm.
    Includes bibliographical references and index.
    ISBN 0-201-61646-7
    1. Java (Computer program language) I. Title.

QA76.73.J38 H34 1999
005.13'3—dc21   99-057905

ISBN 0-201-61646-7
Text printed on recycled and acid-free paper.
1 2 3 4 5 6 7 8 9 10—MA—0403020100
First printing, January 2000

A teacher affects eternity; he can never tell where his influence stops.
—Henry Adams

… in memory of my father.

This book is dedicated to my wife, Tara, and my children, Lauren, Keely, and Andrew.

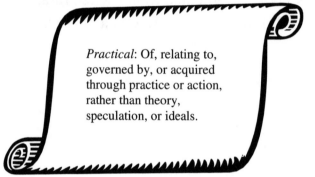

Practical: Of, relating to, governed by, or acquired through practice or action, rather than theory, speculation, or ideals.

Contents

*Praxis: Practice, especially of an art,
science, or technical occupation; opposite to theory.*
—Webster's New Collegiate Dictionary (1958)

Objects and Equality   25

Exception Handling   61

Performance   97

Multithreading   161

Classes and Interfaces 201

Detailed Contents

In theory, there is no difference between theory and practice. But, in practice, there is.
—Jan L.A. van de Snepscheut

All objects in Java are accessed with object references. A common mistake is thinking that Java passes parameters by reference. All parameters are passed by value.

To keep data or an object reference constant, use `final`. Note that `final` only makes the object reference constant, leaving the object free to change.

By default, all non-`static` methods can be overridden by subclasses. Using `final` prevents a subclass from overriding a method.

Arrays and vectors are common storage classes. Know their functionality and characteristics before choosing which to use.

Simply because two methods are declared `synchronized` does not necessarily
mean they are thread safe. Synchronizing on an instance method or object reference obtains a completely different lock than synchronizing on a `static` method
or class literal.

Failure to properly protect data allows users to bypass your synchronization
mechanisms.

By default, do not synchronize all methods. Synchronization is slow and eliminates concurrency. Use the multiple lock per object technique to allow for more
concurrency.

Atomic operations do not automatically mean thread-safe operations. JVM implementations are allowed to keep working copies of variables in private memory. This can lead to stale values. To avoid this problem, use synchronization or
declare variables `volatile`.

Synchronizing a method does not necessarily make the code thread safe. When
`synchronized` methods operate on multiple objects that are not part of the `pri-
vate` instance data of the method's class, you must synchronize on the objects
themselves.

When synchronizing multiple objects, avoid deadlock by acquiring locks in a
fixed, global order.

The `notify` method wakes up only one thread. To wake up multiple threads, use
`notifyAll`.

Preface

Let ignorance talk as it will, learning has its value.
—J. de La Fontaine, *The Use of Knowledge*, Book viii, Fable 19

THIS book is a collection of practical suggestions, advice, examples, and discussion about programming in the Java language. It is organized into individual lessons, each called a PRAXIS (pronounced prak-sis) and each discussing a particular topic. Each PRAXIS is written so that it stands on its own. You can read the book from front to back or select topics individually. This arrangement allows you to read the book in short intervals. Many PRAXES (pronounced prak-sees) are fewer than five pages, thereby allowing you to study them in a brief amount of time.

In the book, I examine in detail particular design and programming issues. I chose the topics based on their relevancy to effective and efficient programming practices. One of the biggest complaints about Java is performance, so I devote the largest section of the book to this topic, exploring techniques to make Java code execute more efficiently.

I wrote this book as a guide to help you design and write code. It helps you understand Java more completely and enables you to write more-efficient, more-robust, and perhaps most important, more-correct code.

All of the information in this book applies to your Java programming. It is not particular to server, client, or GUI (graphical user interface) programming. In addition, you can apply this information to all versions and releases of Java.

The book's style was influenced by Scott Meyers' *Effective C++* and *More Effective C++* books.[1] Because I found his style so useful as a way to organize a book, I decided to adopt a similar format.

Target Audience

This book is intended for Java programmers who already have grasped the basics of the language. It assumes the reader has a working knowledge of Java and concurrent programming and understands object-oriented concepts and terms. It is for the programmer who wants practical advice, discussion, and examples for using the language effectively.

This book provides seasoned Java programmers as well as programmers new to the language with information and discussion regarding key areas of Java. Enough new information is presented that experienced programmers will greatly benefit and be rewarded by looking at areas that they already know. For example, in some cases I discuss a familiar topic in a way that can help a programmer think about it differently or see another side to it not previously explored.

Programmers new to Java can also gain a lot from this book. I offer discussions and examples that help eliminate many common programming errors. I also dispel some common misconceptions about Java and highlight certain questions about specific language features.

Organization of This Book

This book is organized into six main sections.

1. **General Techniques**—Presents several fundamental areas of Java programming including parameter passing, arrays, `Vectors`, and garbage collection.

2. **Objects and Equality**—Examines objects and primitive types and how and why you should implement an `equals` method for a class.

---

[1] *Effective C++: 50 Specific Ways to Improve Your Programs and Designs, Second Edition*, Scott Meyers, Addison-Wesley, 1998. *More Effective C++: 35 New Ways to Improve Your Programs and Designs*, Scott Meyers, Addison-Wesley, 1996.

3. **Exception Handling**—Gives a detailed analysis of exception handling techniques and how to incorporate exceptions into your code effectively.

4. **Performance**—Shows many techniques that you can use to improve the performance of your code. The JVM (Java Virtual Machine), bytecode, and JITs (Just-in-Time code generators) are examined.

5. **Multithreading**—Covers aspects of the threading model that are critical to building robust and reliable multithreaded programs.

6. **Classes and Interfaces**—Explains interfaces and `abstract` and concrete classes and where and when to use each. It also discusses immutable objects, cloning, and finalization in detail.

Under each of these headings is a varied number of related topics. Often, I discuss individual attributes of particular topics in more than one place. For example, I discuss the `synchronized` keyword at length but in various places. Each discussion deals with a different aspect of `synchronized`. However, I have provided extensive cross-referencing so that you will know, when reading a particular topic, where other relevant information exists.

Following the Contents is the Detailed Contents. This section contains all of the PRAXES headings and their page numbers, with a brief summary of the core instruction contained in each PRAXIS. You can use this Detailed Contents to refresh your memory about a topic or to locate a particular topic or subject matter.

The Appendix contains a proven technique to further expand your knowledge about Java. Also included is a Further Reading section, which lists relevant books and periodicals relating to Java and general design and programming.

A Few Words on the Word PRAXIS

PRAXIS is the result of my search for a word that summarizes what I am trying to do in this book. In the 1982 *American Heritage Dictionary*, PRAXIS is defined as follows: *The practical application or exercise of a branch of learning.* This is exactly what I want to do in the book.

The most appropriate definition is provided by *Webster's New Collegiate Dictionary*, 1958: *Practice, especially of an art, science, or technical occupation; opposite to theory.* This definition most accurately sums up what the book is about. The phrase, "opposite to theory," was the clincher. There is nothing wrong with theory. Its place, however, is not in this book.

Example Code

All code examples in the text have been compiled and run with the latest version of Java available when the book was written. The code was compiled and run with the Sun Java 2 SDK, Standard Edition, v1.2.1 on Windows NT 4.0. To access the source code, you must register the book at the following World Wide Web site:

```
http://www.awl.com/cseng/register
```

At this Web site, you will need to enter the unique code found at the back of this book on the page entitled "How to Register Your Book."

Providing Feedback

I welcome feedback on this book. Any comments, criticisms, or bug reports should be sent to `PracticalJava@awl.com`.

I hope you find this book useful, enjoyable, and practical.

Peter Haggar
Research Triangle Park, North Carolina
November, 1999

Acknowledgments

Thank you, good sir, I owe you one.
—George Colman, *The Poor Gentleman*, Act I, Scene ii

WRITING a book is not done alone. Many people contributed their time and energy on my behalf to make this book what it is. Reviewing portions of a manuscript is not an easy task, especially those early manuscript drafts that are, well, early drafts. The patience and willingness to help shown by all of my reviewers are greatly appreciated.

Many people read, reread, and in some cases re-reread portions of the manuscript to provide me with valuable and insightful feedback. The feedback varied from technical to grammatical, and all helped enormously to shape the content and clarity of this book.

Partial drafts of the manuscript were reviewed by Kimberly Bobrow, Joan Boone, Tom Cargill, Bill Field, Dion Gillard, David Hardin, Howard Lee Harkness, Tim Lindholm, George Malek, Jim Mickelson, Devang Patel, Warren Ristow, Susan Elliot Sim, and Dan Trieschman.

Complete drafts of the manuscript were reviewed by Larry Collins, Trevor Cushen, Mary Dageforde, Joshua Engel, Elisabeth Freeman, Cay Horstmann, Susanne Hupfer, Brian Kernighan, Bob Love, Judy Oakley, Linda Rochelle, Clayton Sims, Robert Stanger, and Steve Vinoski.

Although I have been fortunate to have excellent reviewers, I take sole responsibility for any errors remaining herein.

ACKNOWLEDGMENTS

The entire team at Addison-Wesley has been a reliable and guiding force during the creation of this book. They provided invaluable assistance and encouragement throughout, and for that I am indebted to them. They include my editor, Mike Hendrickson, Julie DeBaggis, Tracy Russ, and Jacquelyn Doucette.

I also want to thank my managers at IBM, Carolyn Ruby and John Feller, for their support during the writing of this book.

Special thanks to Rosemary Simpson for her expert work in the creation of a first-rate index.

I must also thank Wayne Kovsky, creator of the Colorado Software Summit Java conference. It is through my association with his conference as a speaker that I honed many of my ideas and became inspired to undertake this project.

Also, thanks to Larry, David, and Mark, who make up the rest of my golfing foursome, for their patience during my many absences over the past several months. To their credit, they have reserved my spot in the group, to which I eagerly return.

As with any project, a few people stand out. They are the ones who go above and beyond, are always there to help, and during the writing of this book, did not seem to have the word no in their vocabularies. Anytime I asked for help or advice or to have yet another PRAXIS I had rewritten reviewed again, they always took the time out of their busy schedules to help.

First, in addition to providing excellent technical reviews, Bob Love always provided the right perspective and was not averse to setting me straight when I veered off course. He, along with Judy Oakley and Robert Stanger, was invaluable during the creation of PRAXES 11 through 15. Clayton Sims, as well as undertaking reviews, provided endless enthusiasm and encouragement while this book was written. Extra thanks are also due to Larry Collins for his ongoing support and help with many aspects of the book. His interminable encouragement and willingness to help, at any hour, are appreciated. Bob, Clayton, and Larry also were generous with their ears, which I excessively bent on more than one occasion.

Most important, I must thank the other four people who endured the most during this endeavor: my wife, Tara, and three young children, Lauren, Keely, and Andrew.

Finally, I want to acknowledge my oldest child Lauren, who learned to read while I wrote this book. My "story," as she calls it, is finally done.

Individual PRAXIS Acknowledgments

Some people do not know they helped. They are the ones whose ideas I read while researching the content of this book. Following is a list of the people and their work that gave me specific ideas for individual PRAXES.

PRAXIS 8 was inspired by Sherman Alpert's article, "Primitive Types Considered Harmful," in the November 1998 issue of *Java Report*.

PRAXIS 12 was influenced by the paper, "Java Cookbook: Porting C++ to Java," by Mark Davis. This paper is found at

    http://www.ibm.com/java/education/portingc/index.html

PRAXES 11 through 15 were greatly influenced by numerous and lengthy discussions and e-mails with Bob Love and Robert Stanger.

After my article, "Effective Exception Handling in Java," appeared in the April 1999 issue of *Java Report*, I received e-mail from Prescott Sanders, Rick Kitts, and Brian Dellert. Prescott and Rick provided suggestions for clarifications of finally block processing, which is included in PRAXIS 22. Brian suggested the information about turning off the JIT, which appears in PRAXIS 23.

PRAXIS 27 was inspired by Tom Cargill's article, "Exception Handling: A False Sense of Security," in the November-December 1994 issue of *C++ Report*.

PRAXIS 33 was inspired by Item 32 of Scott Meyers' *Effective C++, Second Edition* (Addison-Wesley).

PRAXIS 35 was inspired by Paul van Keep's "Java Performance" presentation given at the 1998 Colorado Software Summit Java conference in Keystone, Colorado.

PRAXIS 38 was influenced by the article, "Java: Memories Are Made of This," by Alex McManus in the November 1998 issue of *Java Report*.

PRAXIS 39 was inspired by a presentation given by Kevin Clark at the 1998 ChicagoLand Java Users Group.

PRAXIS 43 contains a discussion of lazy evaluation and some code examples that are based on Item 17 of Scott Meyers' *More Effective C++* (Addison-Wesley).

PRAXES 49, 51, and 52 offer advice based on Jonathan Amsterdam's "Really Understanding Java Threads" presentation given at the 1999 SIGS Object Expo conference in New York, New York.

PRAXIS 54 was inspired by Alan Holub's article, "Programming Java threads in the real world, Part 2," in the October 1998 *JavaWorld*. This article is found at

```
http://www.javaworld.com/javaworld/jw-10-1998/jw-10-toolbox.html
```

PRAXIS 56 was inspired by the article, "Multithreaded assignment surprises," by Steve Ball and John Miller Crawford in the September 1998 issue of *Java Report*.

PRAXES 59 and 60 were influenced by Dion Gillard's "Interfaces and Multiple Inheritance in Java" presentation given at the 1997 Colorado Software Summit Java conference in Keystone, Colorado.

PRAXIS 67 was inspired by several conversations with Bill Field.

General Techniques

You can get by on charm for about 15 minutes.
After that, you better know something.
—H. Jackson Brown, Jr., *Live and Learn and Pass It On*

THIS section covers several fundamental areas of Java programming. It details aspects of Java that need additional explanation and emphasis in order to ensure correct and understandable code. `Vectors` and arrays, two common programming constructs, are analyzed and compared. In addition, language features such as `final` and `instanceof` are discussed and examples and suggested usage included.

This section also discusses the one and only parameter passing mechanism in Java: *pass by value*. It is sometimes assumed that because Java manipulates object references that parameters are likewise passed by reference. This section addresses this wrong assumption. It also explores garbage collection and gives a technique that you can use to help facilitate better memory usage.

PRAXIS 1: Understand that parameters are passed by value, not by reference

A common misconception exists that parameters in Java are passed by reference. They are not. Parameters are passed by value. The misconception arises from the fact that all object variables are object references. (See PRAXIS 8 for detailed information on object references.) This leads to some unexpected results if you do not understand exactly what is happening. For example:

```
import java.awt.Point;
class PassByValue
{
```

```
    public static void modifyPoint(Point pt, int j)
    {
      pt.setLocation(5,5);                                        //1
      j = 15;
      System.out.println("During modifyPoint " + "pt = " + pt +
                         " and j = " + j);
    }

    public static void main(String args[])
    {
      Point p = new Point(0,0);                                   //2
      int i = 10;
      System.out.println("Before modifyPoint " + "p = " + p +
                         " and i = " + i);
      modifyPoint(p, i);                                          //3
      System.out.println("After modifyPoint " + "p = " + p +
                         " and i = " + i);
    }
  }
```

This code creates a Point object, initialized to (0,0), and assigns it to the object reference variable p at //2. It then assigns the primitive int i the value 10. The static modifyPoint method is then called at //3, passing p and i. The modify-Point method calls the setLocation method on the first parameter, pt, changing its location to (5,5). In addition, the second parameter, j, is assigned the value 15. When the modifyPoint method returns, method main prints the values for p and i. What is the output of this code and why?

The output of this code is as follows:

```
    Before modifyPoint p = java.awt.Point[x=0,y=0] and i = 10
    During modifyPoint pt = java.awt.Point[x=5,y=5] and j = 15
    After modifyPoint p = java.awt.Point[x=5,y=5] and i = 10
```

This output shows that the modifyPoint method changes the Point object created at //2 but not the int i. In main, i is assigned the value 10. Parameters are passed by value, therefore, a copy of i is passed to the modifyPoint method. This method changes the value of the copy to 15 and returns. The original value, i in main, is not changed.

By contrast, you might think the Point object created at //2 is unmodified by the modifyPoint method. After all, Java passes parameters by value. Therefore, when modifyPoint is called with the Point object created at //2, a copy is made for the modifyPoint method to work with. Changes to the Point object in modifyPoint are not reflected in `main` because there are two different objects. Right? Wrong.

Actually, `modifyPoint` is working with a copy of a *reference* to the `Point` object, not a copy of the `Point` object. Remember that `p` is an object reference and that Java passes parameters by value. More specifically, Java passes object *references* by value. When `p` is passed from `main` to `modifyPoint`, a copy of the value of `p`, the reference, is passed. Therefore, the `modifyPoint` method is working with the same object but through the alias, `pt`. After entering `modifyPoint`, but before the execution of the code at //1, the object looks like this:

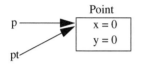

Therefore, after the code at //1 is executed, the `Point` object has changed to (5, 5). What if you want to disallow changes to the `Point` object in methods such as `modifyPoint`? There are two solutions for this:

- Pass a clone of the `Point` object to the `modifyPoint` method. See PRAXES 64 and 66 for more details on cloning.

- Make the `Point` object immutable. See PRAXIS 65 for a discussion of immutable object techniques.

PRAXIS 2:   Use `final` for constant data and constant object references

Many languages offer a notion of *constant data*, which is data that does not change and cannot be changed. Java provides the keyword `final` to specify constant data. For example:

```
class Test
{
    static final int someInt = 10;
    //...
}
```

This code declares an instance variable named `someInt` and sets its value to `10`.

Code that tries to modify the value of someInt does not compile. For example:

```
//...
someInt = 9;   //ERROR
//...
```

The final keyword prevents the unintended mutation of instance data in classes. However, what happens when we want a constant object? For example:

```
class Circle
{
  private double rad;

  public Circle(double r)
  {
    rad = r;
  }

  public void setRadius(double r)
  {
    rad = r;
  }

  public double radius()
  {
    return rad;
  }
}

public class FinalTest
{
  private static final Circle wheel = new Circle(5.0);

  public static void main(String args[])
  {
    System.out.println("Radius of wheel is " +
                          wheel.radius());
    wheel.setRadius(7.4);
    System.out.println("Radius of wheel is now " +
                          wheel.radius());
  }
}
```

The output of this code is:

```
Radius of wheel is 5.0
Radius of wheel is now 7.4
```

In the first example, the compiler generated an error when we tried to change the value of `final` data. In the second, the code compiled cleanly even though the code "changed the value" of the instance variable `wheel`. How can the `wheel` object change values when we specifically declared it `final`?

We did not change the *value* of the variable `wheel`. We changed the content of the object that `wheel` references. But `wheel` was not changed—it still refers to the same object. The variable `wheel` is an object reference into the heap where the object exists. (For more on object references, see PRAXIS 8.) Given this, what happens if we try the following code?

```
public class FinalTest
{
  private static final Circle wheel = new Circle(5.0);

  public static void main(String args[])
  {
    System.out.println("Radius of wheel is " +
                        wheel.radius());
    wheel = new Circle(7.4);
    System.out.println("Radius of wheel is now " +
                        wheel.radius());
  }
}
```

Compiling this code results in what we expect. The following compiler error is generated:

```
FinalTest.java:9: Can't assign a value to a final variable: wheel
    wheel = new Circle(7.4);
    ^
1 error
```

This example generates a compiler error because we attempted to change the *value* of the `final` variable `wheel`. In other words, there is an attempt to change the object to which `wheel` refers. The variable `wheel` is `final` and therefore *immutable*. It must always refer to the same object. However, the object that `wheel` refers to is not affected by the keyword `final` and thus is *mutable*.

The keyword `final` keeps only the value of a variable from changing. If the variable that is declared `final` also happens to be an object reference, the reference cannot be changed and the variable must always refer to the same object. The object referred to, however, is free to change. Declaring objects that are immutable is the subject of PRAXES 63 through 65.

PRAXIS 3: Understand that all non-static methods can be overridden by default

By default, all non-static methods of classes can be overridden by subclasses. The programmer of the class must take specific action in order to prevent subclasses from overriding, and thus changing, the behavior of a method. Subclasses can override any non-static methods unless the methods are declared final.

The final keyword is overloaded in Java. It can be used on instance variables (see PRAXIS 2), on classes, or on methods to indicate that they cannot be overridden. For example:

```
class Base
{
  public void foo()
  {}
  public final void bar()
  {}
}

class Derived extends Base
{
  public void foo()
  {
    //Overriding Base.foo()
  }
  public void bar()
  {
    //Attempting to override Base.bar()
  }
}
```

Compiling this code results in the following error message:

```
Derived.java:15: The method void bar() declared in class Derived
cannot override the final method of the same signature declared in
class Base.  Final methods cannot be overridden.
  public void bar()
            ^
1 error
```

Because the `bar` method in class `Base` is declared `final`, subclasses are not allowed to override it. This is important in two areas:

- Class design
- Runtime performance

You might want to disallow subclasses from altering the behavior of a method. For example, consider a class that represents a particular component on the screen. This class contains a `draw` method that draws the component. The appearance of this component must not change because there are strict requirements on the application. You have two options to prevent users of this class from changing the implementation of `draw`:

1. Declare the class `final`.
2. Declare the `draw` method `final`.

Declaring a class `final` implicitly declares all methods of the class `final`. This prohibits the class from being subclassed, thus disallowing all methods in the class from being overridden. If this is too restrictive for your design, consider declaring only the `draw` method `final`. This allows the class to be subclassed and any of its non-`final` methods to be overridden. In both cases, the `draw` method cannot be changed by a subclass and its implementation is guaranteed not to change.

Use `final` in this manner as an effective tool as you design your classes. Before declaring a class `final`, consider the implications to derived classes and the restrictions this places on them. Performance implications also must be considered with regard to `final` or non-`final` methods. The details of this are covered in PRAXIS 36.

PRAXIS 4:   **Choose carefully between arrays and `Vectors`**

In almost any Java code you write, you will likely use an array of some sort. Java provides two constructs, an array and a `Vector`, which appear to be similar. In fact, the array and `Vector` are altogether different, and it is important that you know the facts about each before choosing which to use in your implementation.

Java arrays have much in common with arrays you might be familiar with from other languages. They also have added benefits. For example, after creating an array you cannot add more elements than the size of the array. In Java, if you add more elements than the size of the array, an `ArrayIndexOutOfBoundsException` is generated at runtime. This differs from other languages, in which this error is not flagged by the runtime environment and thus typically has catastrophic results.

The pointer arithmetic that works with arrays in other languages is not supported for Java arrays. Arrays in Java are objects, so any methods contained in `java.lang.Object` can be invoked on an array. To find the length of an array, you do not call a method. Instead, you use the public variable, `length`. For example, the following code prints the length of the array, `ia`:

```
int[] ia = new int[N];
System.out.println("ia length is " + ia.length);
```

Arrays can hold both primitive types and object references. (See PRAXIS 8 for a discussion of how reference and primitive types differ.) When creating an array, be aware that each array entry is set to its default value based on its type. The following table shows the default values for arrays based on type.

Table 1: Default array values based on type

Type	Default value
boolean	false
char	'\u0000'
byte	0
short	0
int	0
long	0
float	0.0
double	0.0
object reference	null

Java does not invoke a default constructor for array elements that happen to be object references. Instead, all are initialized to `null`. The following code creates an `int` array and an array of `Button` objects. It prints out the values of the array elements after the array has been created but before any initial values are assigned. The array elements are then printed out after they are initialized.

```
    import java.awt.Button;

    class ArrayTest
    {
      public static final int arraySize = 3;
      public static void main(String args[])
      {
        int[] ia = new int[arraySize];
        for (int i=0; i<arraySize; i++)
          System.out.println("int array initially " + ia[i]);

        for (int i=0; i<arraySize; i++)
          ia[i]=i+1;

        for (int i=0; i<arraySize; i++)
          System.out.println("int array now " + ia[i]);

        Button[] oa = new Button[arraySize];
        for (int i=0; i<arraySize; i++)
          System.out.println("Button array initially " + oa[i]);

        for (int i=0; i<arraySize; i++)
          oa[i]=new Button("button " + (i+1));

        for (int i=0; i<arraySize; i++)
          System.out.println("Button array now " + oa[i]);
      }
    }
```

This code produces the following output:

```
    int array initially 0
    int array initially 0
    int array initially 0
    int array now 1
    int array now 2
    int array now 3
    Button array initially null
    Button array initially null
    Button array initially null
    Button array now
    java.awt.Button[button0,0,0,0x0,invalid,label=button 1]
    Button array now
    java.awt.Button[button1,0,0,0x0,invalid,label=button 2]
    Button array now
    java.awt.Button[button2,0,0,0x0,invalid,label=button 3]
```

A Vector, on the other hand, differs significantly from an array in that it grows its size dynamically when more elements are added than its current size can accommodate. Moreover, when elements are removed from a Vector, each element with an index greater than the index being removed is shifted downward to have an index one smaller than the value it had previously.

Unlike arrays, you call a method on a Vector to determine its size. The Vector class implements a size method, which returns the number of elements contained in the Vector. The size method might not return the result you expect, however. Because the size method returns the number of elements contained in a Vector, removing an element changes its size. On the other hand, an array is fixed in size. Its length is the same regardless of how many array indexes have been assigned values.

A Vector is implemented in terms of an array. That is, when you create a Vector the class creates an array of elements of type java.lang.Object to manage the items you store in the Vector. When a Vector grows, its entire array must be reallocated and copied. In addition, when an item is removed from a Vector, its underlying array is compacted. These attributes of the Vector class, coupled with its array implementation, can create performance problems if Vectors are not used properly. See PRAXIS 41 for a detailed analysis of the performance characteristics of arrays and Vectors.

Finally, a Vector may contain only object references and not primitive types. Arrays, by contrast, may contain both object references and primitive types. This restriction is because the Vector class uses an array of type java.lang.Object as its supporting data structure. For example, compiling the following code:

```java
import java.util.Vector;
import java.awt.Button;
class VecArray
{
  public static void main(String args[])
  {
    int i = 1;
    int[] ia = new int[10];
    ia[0] = i;                    //OK

    Button[] ba = new Button[10];
    ba[0] = new Button("");       //OK
    Vector v = new Vector(10);
    v.add(new Button(""));        //OK
    v.add(i);                     //ERROR
    v.add(new Integer(i));        //OK
  }
}
```

results in this output:

```
VecArray.java:15: Incompatible type for method. Can't convert int
to java.lang.Object.
    v.add(i);                        //ERROR
         ^
1 error
```

All elements added to a `Vector` must be of type `java.lang.Object` or one of its subtypes. For this code to work properly, the line causing the error needs to be replaced with this:

```
v.add(new Integer(i));
```

If you are working with a primitive type, consider using an array instead of a Vector. Using an array with primitive types is much more efficient than a `Vector`. (See PRAXES 38 and 41 for detailed information about the performance characteristics of arrays, `Vectors`, and primitive types.) The characteristics of arrays and `Vectors` should be evaluated when choosing which is right for your design and implementation. The following table summarizes the key differences between arrays and `Vectors`.

Table 2: Comparison of array and Vector

	Support for primitive types	Support for objects	Auto size	Fast
array	Yes	Yes	No	Yes
Vector	No	Yes	Yes	No

PRAXIS 5:   Prefer polymorphism to instanceof

Java provides the `instanceof` operator as a mechanism to determine, at runtime, the class to which an object belongs.[1] Like other language features, `instanceof` is often misused. You can avoid many common misuses of `instanceof` by using polymorphism. This is not necessarily done for the object-oriented purity of your code. There are code extensibility reasons to consider as well.

---

[1] This is commonly called the object's *runtime type*.

Suppose that you have the task of writing classes for a payroll system at your company. Consider the following class hierarchy and code:

```
interface Employee
{
  public int salary();
}

class Manager implements Employee
{
  private static final int mgrSal = 40000;
  public int salary()
  {
    return mgrSal;
  }
}

class Programmer implements Employee
{
  private static final int prgSal = 50000;
  private static final int prgBonus = 10000;
  public int salary()
  {
    return prgSal;
  }

  public int bonus()
  {
    return prgBonus;
  }
}

class Payroll
{
  public int calcPayroll(Employee emp)
  {
    int money = emp.salary();
    if (emp instanceof Programmer)
      money += ((Programmer)emp).bonus();  //Calculate the bonus
    return money;
  }

  public static void main(String args[])
  {
    Payroll pr = new Payroll();
    Programmer prg = new Programmer();
    Manager mgr = new Manager();
    System.out.println("Payroll for Programmer is " +
                       pr.calcPayroll(prg));
```

```
    System.out.println("payroll for Manager is " +
                       pr.calcPayroll(mgr));
  }
}
```

Based on this design, the `calcPayroll` method must use the `instanceof` operator to compute the correct result. Because the `calcPayroll` method uses the `Employee interface`, it must figure out to which class the `Employee` object belongs. Because programmers get bonuses and managers do not, you need to determine the runtime type of the `Employee` object.

This is a clear example of using `instanceof` where you can use polymorphism instead. There is no reason to use `instanceof`. What if you want to add another type of `Employee`? Assume you need to add an `Executive` class to your system. With the current design, you must change the implementation of the `calcPayroll` method to check also for the "`instanceof`" the `Executive` class.

This design has several problems. First, it is not efficient, elegant, or easily extensible. Second, it also requires that the programmer writing the code do the work of the Java runtime system. You need to call `instanceof` to figure out to which class various objects belong in order to invoke the correct methods. A better way is to let the Java runtime system figure all of this out for you. This generates a cleaner and more elegant design, as well as more efficient and easily understood code.

To avoid these problems, structure the code so that `instanceof` is not needed. You avoid using `instanceof` with polymorphism. Furthermore, with a proper design, the `calcPayroll` method does not have to change with the addition of a new type of `Employee`. A proper design allows the correct methods to be called at all times. To fix these problems, the code looks like this:

```
interface Employee
{
  public int salary();
  public int bonus();
}

class Manager implements Employee
{
  private static final int mgrSal = 40000;
  private static final int mgrBonus = 0;
  public int salary()
  {
    return mgrSal;
  }
```

```
      public int bonus()
      {
        return mgrBonus;
      }
  }

  class Programmer implements Employee
  {
    private static final int prgSal = 50000;
    private static final int prgBonus = 10000;
    public int salary()
    {
      return prgSal;
    }

    public int bonus()
    {
      return prgBonus;
    }
  }

  class Payroll
  {
    public int calcPayroll(Employee emp)
    {
      //Calculate the bonus. No instanceof check needed.
      return emp.salary() + emp.bonus();
    }

    public static void main(String args[])
    {
      Payroll pr = new Payroll();
      Programmer prg = new Programmer();
      Manager mgr = new Manager();
      System.out.println("Payroll for Programmer is " +
                          pr.calcPayroll(prg));
      System.out.println("Payroll for Manager is " +
                          pr.calcPayroll(mgr));
    }
  }
```

With this design, you eliminate the need to use instanceof by adding the bonus method to your Employee interface. This requires the Programmer and Manager classes, which implement the Employee interface, to implement both the salary and bonus methods. This, in turn, simplifies the calcPayroll method significantly.

There are times, however, when the solution outlined here is not feasible and you must resort to using the `instanceof` operator. Refer again to the initial class hierarchy, assuming this time the `Employee interface` and the `Manager` and `Programmer` classes are all part of a library you are using. Further assume you do not have the ability to modify the source code of this library. Your task is to use this poorly designed library to write the `calcPayroll` method to compute the salary of the different types of `Employees`. In this case, you must either use the `instanceof` operator to correctly write your `calcPayroll` method or create two `calcPayroll` methods, one to accept `Programmer` object references and one to accept `Manager` object references. Neither choice is desirable, but either is necessary if access to the source code is not possible.

The `instanceof` operator can easily be abused. In many cases, polymorphism is used to eliminate the use of `instanceof`. Whenever you see code that uses `instanceof`, determine whether you can refine the design to eliminate it. Refining the design in this way produces a more logical and serviceable design and more maintainable code.

PRAXIS 6:   Use `instanceof` only when you must

In Item 39 of his book *Effective C++*, Scott Meyers proclaims: "Anytime you find yourself writing code of the form, 'if the object is of type T1, then do something, but if it's of type T2, then do something else,' slap yourself."[2] For the majority of cases, Meyers is absolutely right. His sage advice applies equally to Java. There are situations, however, in which you need to write code in this fashion. In these rare instances, you should not slap yourself.

PRAXIS 5 describes an occasional situation in which, through improper class library design, a client of a class could not avoid using `instanceof`. There are more common situations in which you have no other option but to use `instanceof`. For example, sometimes you must downcast from a base to a derived type. Fortunately, Java provides mechanisms that make downcasting safe. A cast done improperly results in either a compile-time error or an exception thrown at runtime.

An invalid cast can generate a compile-time error. An example is casting from one type to an unrelated type. By contrast, an exception is generated when the cast is

---

[2] *Effective C++: 50 Specific Ways to Improve Your Programs and Designs, Second Edition*, Scott Meyers, Addison-Wesley, 1998.

within the same class hierarchy but determined at runtime to be invalid. For example:

```
class Shape
{}
class Circle extends Shape
{}
class Triangle extends Shape
{}
class Polynomial
{}

class Shapes
{
  public static void main(String args[])
  {
    Shape shape1 = new Circle();
    Object shape2 = new Triangle();

    Polynomial poly = (Polynomial)shape1;  //Compile error.
    Triangle tri = (Triangle)shape1;       //Runtime error.
    Triangle tri2 = (Triangle)shape2;      //OK
  }
}
```

The shape1 and shape2 object references are of type Shape and Object, respectively. The shape1 reference refers to an object of the Circle class, and the shape2 reference refers to an object of the Triangle class.

Casting a reference of type Shape to type Polynomial cannot succeed because these objects are not related. The Java compiler detects this and issues a compile-time error message. The cast of a reference of type Shape to type Triangle is at least in the same object hierarchy and is, therefore, potentially valid. The validity of this downcast can be determined only at runtime. The Java runtime checks to see whether the object referenced by shape1 is of class Triangle. Because it is not, a ClassCastException is generated. The last cast is valid because it passes both tests.

You might be inclined to think that you can be careful when you need to cast and can eliminate the need to use instanceof. This is not the case. Consider, for example, the Vector class. A Vector has the property that all objects it contains are stored as type java.lang.Object or one of its subtypes. In addition, an element retrieved from a Vector is returned with the type java.lang.Object. This occurs no matter what the derived type the object was at the time it was stored in the Vector. (All Java objects are derived from java.lang.Object.)

To use the methods of a derived object stored in a `Vector`, you must downcast from `java.lang.Object` to the derived class to which the object belongs. Because Java makes downcasting safe by performing both compile-time and run-time checking, the possibility exists that if the cast is performed incorrectly, the JVM will generate a `ClassCastException` at runtime. To avoid this, you have two options:

1. Use a `try/catch` block to handle the `ClassCastException`.

2. Use the `instanceof` operator.

Option 1, using a `try/catch` block, works but is inadvisable (see PRAXES 23 and 24). Because you can avoid the generation of this exception, a better solution is to use the `instanceof` operator. This ensures a downcast that does not result in a runtime exception. Consider the following code:

```java
import java.util.Vector;

class Shape
{}

class Circle extends Shape
{
  public double radius()
  {
    return 5.7;
  }
  //...
}

class Triangle extends Shape
{
  public boolean isRightTriangle()
  {
    //Code to determine if triangle is right
    return true;
  }
  //...
}

class StoreShapes
{
  public static void main(String args[])
  {
    Vector shapeVector = new Vector(10);
    shapeVector.add(new Triangle());
    shapeVector.add(new Triangle());
```

```
        shapeVector.add(new Circle());
        //...
        //Assume many Triangles and Circles are added and removed
        //...
        int size = shapeVector.size();
        for (int i=0; i<size; i++)
        {
          Object o = shapeVector.get(i);
          if (o instanceof Triangle)
          {
            if (((Triangle)o).isRightTriangle())
            {
              //...
            }
          }
          else if (o instanceof Circle)
          {
            double rad = ((Circle)o).radius();
            //...
          }
        }
      }
    }
```

This code demonstrates where using the `instanceof` operator might be necessary. As the objects are retrieved from the `Vector`, they are of class
`java.lang.Object`. Using `instanceof` determines what class the object
belongs to, thereby allowing the downcast to be performed without the possibility
of an exception being thrown at runtime.

Alternatively, you can store the `Circle` and `Triangle` objects in different `Vec-
tors` and avoid `instanceof`. However, you need to use `instanceof` if you do not
control the contents of a collection such as a `Vector`.

PRAXIS 7:   Set object references to `null` when they are no longer needed

Garbage collection in Java reclaims memory that is no longer in use without the
programmer's having to explicitly call methods to free the memory. For this reason, methods such as `free` and `delete` are unnecessary, and the Java language
does not provide them. The existence of garbage collection leads some programmers to ignore memory issues. Not concerning yourself with memory issues is a
mistake. You still need to pay attention to how memory is being used in your code.

The garbage collector frees memory held by an object only if the object is no longer being referenced. You can help the garbage collector free memory by setting certain references to `null` when you are finished with them. This might be especially helpful if your program is running in a memory-constrained environment.

Even with the garbage collector running, all unreferenced memory might not be reclaimed. Depending on the garbage collection algorithm used by the JVM your code runs with, not every unreferenced object is reclaimed on each invocation of the garbage collector. Multiple invocations might be needed to reclaim an unreferenced object. An older, long-lived object is less likely to be unreferenced than is a new object, so a common garbage collection algorithm is to analyze older objects less often than newer objects.

You can figure out some of the behavior of the garbage collector your JVM uses by querying the available memory, calling `System.gc`, and then querying the available memory again:

```
Runtime rt = Runtime.getRuntime();
long mem = rt.freeMemory();
System.out.println("Free Memory is: " + mem);
//...
System.gc();
//...
mem = rt.freeMemory();
System.out.println("Free Memory is now: " + mem);
```

The vast majority of JVM implementations results in the execution of the garbage collector as a result of the `System.gc` method call. In addition, most JVM implementations implicitly invoke the garbage collector when memory is low or when the CPU is idle for a period of time. This time period is dependent on the garbage collection algorithm used by the JVM.

Memory problems can arise when objects contain instance variables that are initialized in the constructor and reference objects that consume large amounts of memory. If such objects exist for a large percentage of the program's runtime and all of the memory that they reference is not needed for this time period, a lot of memory is wasted. This can be detrimental to the performance of your code.

The following example has a `main` method that contains a `Customers` object to provide information for a GUI:

```
class Customers
{
```

```
      private int[] custIdArray;

      public Customers(String db)
      {
        int num = queryDB(db);
        custIdArray = new int[num];
        for (int i=0; i<num; i++)
          custIdArray[i] = //Some value from a database
                           //representing a customer ID.
      }
      //...
    }

    class Foo
    {
      public static void main(String args[])
      {
        Customers cust = new Customers("SomeDataBase");
        //Use our Customers object to prime fields in a GUI.
        //...
        //Customers object no longer needed.
        //...
        //The rest of the app...
      }
    }
```

Assume this particular Customers object is large because it is storing customer IDs for 20,000 customers. Also assume the Customers object exists for the life of the program and is not needed after the GUI is built, which is long before the method exits. Given this, how do you change the code to not use so much memory?

One solution is to set the local variable, cust, to null after the GUI has been built. This removes the reference to the Customers object and might allow the garbage collector to reclaim the memory the next time it runs. With this change, the main method looks like this:

```
    class Foo
    {
      public static void main(String args[])
      {
        Customers cust = new Customers("SomeDataBase");
        //Use our Customers object to prime fields in a GUI.
        //...
        //Customers object no longer needed.
        cust = null;
        //The rest of the app...
      }
    }
```

What if you need to keep the Customers object available for the duration of the program but have limited use for the custIdArray portion of the Customers object after the GUI is built? Sometimes you might need the array in the future, but most often you will not. In this case, you could provide a method on the Customers class that simply sets the custIdArray variable to null and then invoke the method from main:

```
class Customers
{
  private int[] custIdArray;

  public Customers(String db)
  {
    int num = queryDB(db);
    custIdArray = new int[num];
    for (int i=0; i<num; i++)
      custIdArray[i] = //Some value from a database
                       //representing a customer ID.
  }

  public void unrefCust()
  {
    custIdArray = null;
  }
  //...
}

class Foo
{
  public static void main(String args[])
  {
    Customers cust = new Customers("SomeDataBase");
    //Use our Customers object to prime fields in a GUI.
    //...
    //Customers object no longer needed.
    cust.unrefCust();
    //The rest of the app...
  }
}
```

This code has the desired effect of setting the array object reference to null. However, this solution has potential negative implications. In the initial example, the class design is such that the array can be assumed to be present and initialized. The addition of the unrefCust method changes this design. The code now needs to handle the situation in which the array is needed but is no longer valid. You might also need to add methods to reestablish the array after it has been unreferenced.

These techniques can also be used in class methods where local variables might have a brief life span. Do not assume that because the object is unreferenced at the end of the method that it cannot affect your code. Consider this code:

```
public void someMethod()
{
  BigObject bigObj = new BigObject();
  //Use bigObj
  //Done with bigObj
  bigObj = null;
  //Rest of method...
}
```

Setting a local variable reference to null can have advantages. In this example, the bigObj reference is not needed long before the end of the method. Setting it to null might free this memory the next time the garbage collector runs. The garbage collector might run before the method completes. In this case, setting this variable to null might be advantageous if the rest of this method requires large amounts of memory.

These techniques can solve the problem of holding large amounts of unneeded memory. To use as little memory as possible, objects that exist for the life of the program must be as small as possible. In addition, large objects should exist for as brief a time as possible.

Limiting the amount of memory used by a Java program might help the performance only of Java code running in the same instance of the JVM and not necessarily of other programs running on the same system. This is because many heap management algorithms preallocate a piece of memory for use by your code. Assume your JVM preallocates a 12MB heap that never grows. Regardless of the percentage of this heap your program uses, this fact alone does not affect how other system processes run. However, the percentage of the heap your program uses has a direct impact on your program's performance.

When reviewing code, pay attention to large objects, especially those that exist for the lifetime, or great portions, of the program. Study how these objects are created and used and how much memory they might reference. If they reference large amounts of memory, determine if all of the memory is needed during the life of the object. Some large objects possibly can be unreferenced, thereby allowing a more efficient execution of the rest of the code.

At any time, you can request the garbage collector to run by invoking the `System.gc` method. If you unreference an object, you can call `System.gc` to request the garbage collector to run and reclaim the memory before the code proceeds further. Before doing this, you should consider the potential performance impact this can have on your code.

Many garbage collection algorithms suspend all other threads before they run. This ensures that when the garbage collector runs, it has complete access to the memory in the heap and can perform its tasks safely without the threat of being preempted by another thread. When the garbage collector is done with its work, all threads that it suspended before it ran are resumed.

Therefore, by explicitly requesting that the garbage collector run with the `System.gc` method call, you risk delays while it performs a collection. The amount of the delay depends on the garbage collection algorithm used by the JVM.

The garbage collector on most JVMs runs often enough that explicitly invoking it is not necessary. However, you might consider calling `System.gc` if you have areas in your code where you want to free up as much memory as possible before proceeding further.

Objects and Equality

A popular equality reigns here.
—William Wordsworth, *Complete Poetical Works* (1888)

JAVA provides objects, primitive types, and the notion of equality of type. These three elements are an important foundation for your class design. Your usage of objects and primitive types has more impact on your code than you might expect. Furthermore, the notion of equality is often overlooked. Ignoring equality leads to non-intuitive and incorrect behavior of classes and code. Users expect certain semantics with regard to equality of objects.

This section explores the issues surrounding these three important elements and offers guidance regarding their pitfalls, implementation, and usage.

PRAXIS 8: Differentiate between reference and primitive types

Java provides two different types: reference types and primitive, or built-in, types. In addition, wrapper classes are provided for each primitive type. If you need a variable for an integer, do you use the primitive `int` or an object of the `Integer` class? If you need to declare a boolean type, do you use the primitive `boolean` or an object of the `Boolean` class? The following table shows the primitive types along with their object wrapper classes.

Table 3: Primitive types and wrapper classes

Primitive type	Wrapper class
`boolean`	`Boolean`
`char`	`Character`

Table 3: Primitive types and wrapper classes (continued)

Primitive type	Wrapper class
byte	Byte
short	Short
int	Integer
long	Long
float	Float
double	Double

References and primitives behave altogether differently and possess different semantics. For example, assume there are two local variables in a method. One local variable is a primitive of type `int`, and the other is an object reference to an `Integer` object:

```
int i = 5;                   //Primitive type
Integer j = new Integer(10); //Object reference
```

These two variables, which are stored in a local variable table and manipulated on the Java operand stack, are represented completely differently. (For the remainder of this discussion, the generic term *stack* is used in place of operand stack or *local variable table*.) The primitive type `int` and the object reference are each stored on the stack in 32 bits.[1] The stack entry for the `Integer` object is not the object itself but an object reference.

All objects in Java are accessed by object references. Object references are pointers to an area in the heap where the storage for the object exists. When you declare a primitive type, you declare the storage for the type itself. The previous two lines of code are represented like this:

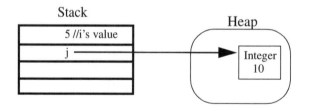

---

[1] JVM implementations, at a minimum, use 32 bits of storage each to represent an `int` and an object reference.

Reference and primitive types have different characteristics and usages. These include size and speed issues (see PRAXIS 38), in what type of data structure the type is stored (see PRAXIS 4), and the default values assigned when references and primitives are used as instance data of a class. The default value for an object reference instance variable is `null`, whereas the default value for a primitive type instance variable varies depending on its type. See Table 1 on page 8 for a list of default values used for instance variables of the different types in Java. (This table also shows the default values for arrays based on type.)

For many programs, the code will contain both primitive types and their object wrappers. Using both of these types and knowing how they correctly interact and coexist is problematic when testing for equality (see PRAXIS 9). Programmers must understand how these types work and interact in order to avoid buggy code.

For example, you cannot call a method on a primitive type, but you can, of course, call a method on an object:

```
int j = 5;
j.hashCode();   //ERROR
//...
Integer i = new Integer(5);
i.hashCode();   //OK
```

Using a primitive type eliminates the need to call new and create an object. This saves time and space (see PRAXIS 38). Mixing primitive types and objects can also create unexpected results with regard to assignment. What looks like innocent code might not do what you expect. For example:

```
import java.awt.Point;

class Assign
{
  public static void main(String args[])
  {
    int a = 1;
    int b = 2;
    Point x = new Point(0,0);
    Point y = new Point(1,1);                                    //1
    System.out.println("a is " + a);
    System.out.println("b is " + b);
    System.out.println("x is " + x);
    System.out.println("y is " + y);
    System.out.println("Performing assignment and " +
                       "setLocation...");
    a = b;
```

```
        a++;
        x = y;                                              //2
        x.setLocation(5,5);                                 //3

        System.out.println("a is " + a);
        System.out.println("b is " + b);
        System.out.println("x is " + x);
        System.out.println("y is " + y);
    }
}
```

This code generates the following output:

```
a is 1
b is 2
x is java.awt.Point[x=0,y=0]
y is java.awt.Point[x=1,y=1]
Performing assignment and setLocation...
a is 3
b is 2
x is java.awt.Point[x=5,y=5]
y is java.awt.Point[x=5,y=5]
```

The results of modifying the integers a and b are not surprising. The integer variable a is assigned the value of b and then a is increased by 1. The output reflects what we expect to happen. What might be surprising, however, is the output of the x and y objects after the assignment and the call to `setLocation`. How can x and y have the same values when we specifically called `setLocation` on x *after* the assignment of x = y? After all, we assigned y to x and then changed x just as we did with the integers a and b.

The confusion is due to the usage of primitive types and objects. Assignment is not doing anything different with these types. It might, however, appear that it is. Assignment makes the value on the left-hand side of the equals (=) sign equal to the value on the right-hand side. This is obvious for primitive types such as the previous `int` a and b. For non-primitive types, such as the `Point` objects, assignment modifies the object reference and not the object. Therefore, after the statement

```
    x = y;
```

x is equal to y. In other words, because x and y are object references, they now refer to the same object. Therefore, any changes to x also change y. Here is what the situation looks like after the code at //1 is executed:

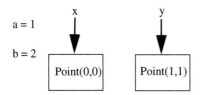

After the assignment at //2, the situation is as follows:

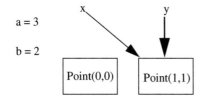

When setLocation is called at //3, the method is executed on the object that x references. Because x references the same Point object as does y, we now have:

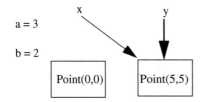

Because x and y refer to the same object, all methods that are executed on x work with the same object as methods that are executed on y.

It is important to distinguish between reference and primitive types and to understand the semantics of references. Failure to do so results in code that does not behave as intended.

PRAXIS 9:   Differentiate between == and equals

Confusion can arise whenever the discussion turns to the question of equality in Java. What is the difference between the == operator and the equals method?

When do you use one over the other? What is the `equals` method anyway? Isn't == good enough?

Failure to understand this issue leads to buggy code. Consider the following example that illustrates the problem:

```
class Test
{
  public static void main(String args[])
  {
    int a = 10;
    int b = 10;
    System.out.println("a==b is " + (a==b));

    Integer ia = new Integer(10);
    Integer ib = new Integer(10);
    System.out.println("ia==ib is " + (ia==ib));
  }
}
```

Running this code generates the following output:

```
a==b is true
ia==ib is false
```

If you are not sure why these results are generated, you might modify this code to the following:

```
class Test
{
  public static void main(String args[])
  {
    int a = 10;
    int b = 10;
    System.out.println("a is " + a);
    System.out.println("b is " + b);
    System.out.println("a==b is " + (a==b));

    Integer ia = new Integer(10);
    Integer ib = new Integer(10);
    System.out.println("ia is " + ia);
    System.out.println("ib is " + ib);
    System.out.println("ia==ib is " + (ia==ib));
  }
}
```

You run it again and generate the following output:

```
a is 10
b is 10
a==b is true
ia is 10
ib is 10
ia==ib is false
```

If it is not clear why this code generates this output, look at it a little more closely. The variables a and b are of type int. They are known as primitive types (see PRAXES 8 and 38) and they have no object associated with them. By contrast, the variables ia and ib are object references and reference Java Integer objects. You might be inclined to say, "So, big deal. They all have the same value of 10." Well, they do and they don't.

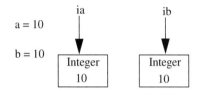

The primitive types, a and b, do have the value of 10. The object references, ia and ib, are really references to two *different* Java Integer objects that have the value 10. Therefore, the values of ia and ib are not 10 but rather unique values that represent the two objects. The == operator simply tests for equality. Is the thing on the left-hand side of the == the same as the thing on the right-hand side? Because ia and ib are references to different objects, they have different values and are therefore not equal.

How do you test to see whether the values referenced by ia and ib are equal? You have seen that the == operator does not give you the result you want, so this is where you use the equals method. The equals method tests for value, or semantic equality. Because it is a method, it can be used only with objects. It cannot be used with primitive types such as int, float, and boolean. Therefore, to test whether ia and ib are equal, the code is written as follows:

```
class Test
{
  public static void main(String args[])
  {
    Integer ia = new Integer(10);
    Integer ib = new Integer(10);
```

```
        System.out.println("ia.equals(ib) is " + (ia.equals(ib)));
        System.out.println("ib.equals(ia) is " + (ib.equals(ia)));
    }
}
```

This code produces the following output:

```
ia.equals(ib) is true
ib.equals(ia) is true
```

Another source of problems with equality is the comparison of different types. Consider the following code:

```
class Test
{
    public static void main(String args[])
    {
        int a = 10;
        float b = 10.0f;
        System.out.println("a is " + a);
        System.out.println("b is " + b);
        System.out.println("a==b is " + (a==b));

        Integer ia = new Integer(10);
        Float fa = new Float(10.0f);
        System.out.println("ia is " + ia);
        System.out.println("fa is " + fa);
        System.out.println("ia.equals(fa) is " + (ia.equals(fa)));
        System.out.println("fa.equals(ia) is " + (fa.equals(ia)));
    }
}
```

The output of this code is the following:

```
a is 10
b is 10.0
a==b is true
ia is 10
fa is 10.0
ia.equals(fa) is false
fa.equals(ia) is false
```

This code shows that two different types of primitives can be equal but two different types of objects are not. When the primitive int a and the primitive float b are compared, the int a is promoted, or widened, to a float. Its value changes from 10 to 10.0, which results in the two values being considered equal. However, two objects of different classes are never considered equal unless a custom implementation of the `equals` method is provided. Doing this, however, is not recommended. For more on `equals` method implementations, see PRAXES 11 through 15.

The bottom line is, use == when testing if two primitive types are identical or if two object references refer to the same object, and use the `equals` method to compare whether two objects are the same based on their attributes. (Comparing objects based on their attributes is also known as testing for value or semantic equality.) Before you jump in and start to use `equals`, see PRAXIS 10, which uncovers some lurking problems.

PRAXIS 10: **Do not rely on the default implementation of `equals`**

PRAXIS 9 explains when to use the == operator and when to use the `equals` method. However, if you call an `equals` method without regard for its implementation, you might not get the result you expect.

For example, assume you are writing software for a golf equipment warehouse. One task is to figure out the number of duplicate balls that are in stock. You might write a class for golf balls that looks like this:

```
class Golfball
{
  private String brand;
  private String make;
  private int compression;

  public Golfball (String str, String mk, int comp)
  {
    brand = str;
    make = mk;
    compression = comp;
  }

  public String brand()
  {
    return brand;
  }

  public String make()
  {
    return make;
  }
```

```
    public int compression()
    {
      return compression;
    }
}
```

Each Golfball object contains the brand, make, and compression for the ball. For two Golfball objects to be equal, these three attributes must all be the same. Further assume that after each Golfball object is created, it is stored in a database. When you later access the database, you need to determine which Golfball objects are the same in order to generate an accurate count. Consider the following code to compare two Golfball objects:

```
class Warehouse
{
  public static void main(String args[])
  {
    Golfball gb1 = new Golfball("BrandX", "Professional", 100);
    Golfball gb2 = new Golfball("BrandX", "Professional", 100);
    //...
    if (gb1.equals(gb2))
      System.out.println("Ball 1 equals Ball 2");
    else
      System.out.println("Ball 1 does not equal Ball 2");
  }
}
```

You know for the ball count calculation to work as you designed it, you must use equals and not == (see PRAXIS 9). However, to your surprise, when you run this code, you find that none of your Golfball objects are ever equal. In this example, the output is as follows:

```
Ball 1 does not equal Ball 2
```

This implementation results in every ball being considered different. "Wait a minute," you say, "I just finished reading PRAXIS 9, and there you told me to use the equals method for this type of comparison, and now it doesn't work." Yes, you are supposed to use the equals method because == simply compares the object references. Moreover, you know that all of the object references are different because all of the Golfball objects are unique. Here is the question to ask: "What equals method is being invoked?" As you might have guessed, it is not the one you want.

You might now wonder why the code in PRAXIS 9 produced the correct result and the previous code did not. The code in PRAXIS 9 calls equals on an Integer object. Because the Integer class provides its own implementation of equals, this method was used. In the previous example, equals is called on a Golfball object that does not implement its own, therefore, the equals method of java.lang.Object is used.

All Java classes implicitly inherit from java.lang.Object, Java's base Object class. The Golfball class is no exception. In addition, because the Golfball class does not implement its own equals method, you are implicitly using the equals method implementation of java.lang.Object. This method is implemented as follows:

```
public boolean equals(Object obj)
{
   return (this == obj);
}
```

The Warehouse class's code executes the equals method of java.lang.Object for each Golfball object. This default implementation of the equals method does exactly what you *do not* want it to do: It checks whether the object references refer to the same object.[2] The java.lang.Object version of the equals method is analogous to coding the test like this:

```
if (gb1 == gb2)
//...
```

You know this is never true for this example. What you want to know is whether the brand, make, and compression of the balls are the same. Fixing this problem requires the Golfball class to implement its own equals method and not rely on the default implementation supplied by java.lang.Object.

```
class Golfball
{
   //As before...
   public boolean equals(Object obj)
   {
```

[2.] You might wonder why java.lang.Object provides this method. If it did not, code that calls equals on an object that does not have an equals method implementation would generate a compiler error, not the incorrect result. Because its implementation compares only object references, it is easily replaced by code of the form:
`if (obj1 == obj2)`.

```
      if (this == obj)
        return true;

      if (obj != null && getClass() == obj.getClass())
      {
        Golfball gb = (Golfball)obj;  //Classes are equal, downcast.
        if (brand.equals(gb.brand()) &&  //Compare attributes.
            make.equals(gb.make()) &&
            compression == gb.compression())
        {
          return true;
        }
      }
      return false;
    }
  }
```

Running your code with this implementation of the equals method in the Golf-ball class produces the desired and correct results:

```
Ball 1 equals Ball 2
```

Keep in mind that you do not have to check all of the fields of the object. You have to check only the fields necessary to determine if two objects are equal, according to your design. For example, you might decide that two Golfball objects are equal if their brand and make attributes are the same, regardless of their compression. You would then remove the ball compression check in your implementation of the equals method.

Also notice that the equals method implementation is careful to use the == operator on the primitive compression attribute and the equals method on the String object reference variables. This ensures that an accurate result is generated (see PRAXIS 9).

Everything is fine with your design, and the code works fine at the golf equipment warehouse. One day, some of your programmers decide (after reading PRAXIS 31 of a book called *Practical Java* they recently purchased) to change the brand and make fields of the Golfball object to use StringBuffer instead of String. The Golfball class now looks like this:

```
class Golfball
{
  private StringBuffer brand;
  private StringBuffer make;
  private int compression;
```

```
    public Golfball (StringBuffer str, StringBuffer mk, int comp)
    {
      brand = str;
      make = mk;
      compression = comp;
    }

    public StringBuffer brand()
    {
      return brand;
    }

    public StringBuffer make()
    {
      return make;
    }
    //As before...
}
```

This seems like an innocent enough change to the class. You have not changed the equals method, only other parts of the Golfball class. The Golfball class has simply changed from using the String class to using a StringBuffer. When you test your new Golfball class, you might be surprised to find that it does not work. Running the test program produces the following output:

```
Ball 1 does not equal Ball 2
```

What is happening here? You added the equals method earlier to make this work. Now it is broken again, and you did not even change the equals method. All you did was change from String to StringBuffer. Certainly that could not have caused the problem. Well, it did.

Look again at the equals method. Notice that it calls an equals method itself. This is your red flag. What equals method does it call? It calls the equals method of the brand and make objects. In the previous example, those objects were of type String, and thus the equals method used was that of the String class. Now they are of type StringBuffer. Therein lies the problem.

The Java String class correctly implements an equals method. The Java StringBuffer class, however, does not implement one at all. Because the StringBuffer class does not implement an equals method—you guessed it— the java.lang.Object equals method is used. And because the superclass of StringBuffer is java.lang.Object, this makes sense. We saw earlier in this

PRAXIS, however, why the `java.lang.Object` equals method did not work. It was also the reason you wrote your own `equals` method to begin with.

There are several solutions to this problem:

1. Return to using a `String` object.

2. Modify the `equals` method of `Golfball` to convert the `StringBuffer` objects to `String` objects before calling `equals`.

3. Write your own `StringBuffer` class that includes an `equals` method.

4. Forgo the `equals` methods, and write your own `compare` method that compares two `StringBuffer` objects for equality.

Option 1 is the simplest solution: Return to using the `String` class. You know that it works and involves the least amount of work. Depending on your implementation, however, you might prefer to use a `StringBuffer` for the `brand` and `make` fields of your `Golfball` object (see PRAXIS 31).

Option 2, using `StringBuffer`, is to modify the `equals` method of the `Golfball` class to convert the `StringBuffer` objects to `String` objects. Doing so guarantees that the `equals` method of `String` is called for the comparison—this ensures the correct result. The modified `Golfball` class using this technique looks like this:

```
class Golfball
{
  //As before...
  public boolean equals(Object obj)
  {
    if (this == obj)
      return true;

    if (obj != null && getClass() == obj.getClass())
    {
      Golfball gb = (Golfball)obj;  //Classes are equal, downcast.
      if (brand.toString().equals(gb.brand().toString()) &&
          make.toString().equals(gb.make().toString()) &&
          compression == gb.compression())
      {
        return true;
      }
    }
    return false;
  }
}
```

This solution works and generates the correct results when your test code is run. However, it might be too costly for your implementation. Calls to the toString method on a StringBuffer object result in a new String object being created each time, which is costly (see PRAXIS 32). This does, however, solve the problem initially created by the use of StringBuffer.

Option 3 is to create your own StringBuffer class and implement the equals method for this class yourself. Before implementing your own equals method, see PRAXES 11 through 15. This involves a bit more work, but it allows you to take advantage of StringBuffer.

The following is a class called MyStringBuffer that utilizes the "has-a," or containment, relationship with StringBuffer. This design is required because StringBuffer is a final class and classes that are final cannot be extended. Therefore, a MyStringBuffer object contains a reference to an instance of a StringBuffer object. The implementation of MyStringBuffer looks like this:

```java
class MyStringBuffer
{
  private StringBuffer stringbuf;

  public MyStringBuffer(String str)
  {
    stringbuf = new StringBuffer(str);
  }

  public int length()
  {
    return stringbuf.length();
  }

  public synchronized char charAt(int index)
  {
    return (stringbuf.charAt(index));
  }
  //Create passthrough methods for the rest of the
  //StringBuffer methods as needed.

  public boolean equals(Object obj)
  {
    if (this == obj)
      return true;

    if (obj != null && getClass() == obj.getClass())
    {
      MyStringBuffer sb = (MyStringBuffer)obj; //Classes equal,
      int len = length();                      //downcast.
```

```
    if (len != sb.length())  //If lengths are not equal, strings
      return false;           //can't be either.

    int index = 0;
    while(index != len)  //Compare the strings.
    {
      if (charAt(index) != sb.charAt(index))
        return false;
      else
        index++;
    }
    return true;
  }
  return false;
}
}
```

The Golfball class using the MyStringBuffer class looks like this:

```
class Golfball
{
  private MyStringBuffer brand;
  private MyStringBuffer make;
  private int compression;

  public Golfball (MyStringBuffer str,
                   MyStringBuffer mk, int comp)
  {
    brand = str;
    make = mk;
    compression = comp;
  }

  public MyStringBuffer brand()
  {
    return brand;
  }

  public MyStringBuffer make()
  {
    return make;
  }

  public int compression()
  {
    return compression;
  }
```

```
    public boolean equals(Object obj)
    {
      if (this == obj)
        return true;

      if (obj != null && getClass() == obj.getClass())
      {
        Golfball gb = (Golfball)obj;  //Classes are equal, downcast.
        if (brand.equals(gb.brand()) &&  //Compare attributes.
            make.equals(gb.make()) &&
            compression == gb.compression())
        {
          return true;
        }
      }
      return false;
    }
    //...
}
```

Finally, the Warehouse class using the MyStringBuffer class looks like this:

```
class Warehouse
{
  public static void main(String args[])
  {
    Golfball gb1 = new Golfball(
                new MyStringBuffer("BrandX"),
                new MyStringBuffer("Professional"), 100);
    Golfball gb2 = new Golfball(
                new MyStringBuffer("BrandX"),
                new MyStringBuffer("Professional"), 100);
    //...
    if (gb1.equals(gb2))
      System.out.println("Ball 1 equals Ball 2");
    else
      System.out.println("Ball 1 does not equal Ball2");
  }
}
```

This code produces the desired output:

```
Ball 1 equals Ball 2
```

Option 4 involves writing a static compare method that compares two String-Buffer objects for equality. The equals method of the Golfball class must change to call the compare method instead of the equals method. The implementation of the compare method is similar to the equals method of the MyStringBuffer class.

This solution has the benefit that you do not need to create another class to provide a way to compare two StringBuffer objects. However, its drawback is that you must change the equals method of the Golfball class to call the compare method instead of an equals method. This means that if you later decide to return to using a String object, the equals method of the Golfball class must change as well. For example, the static compare method and the equals method of Golfball look like this:

```java
class Golfball
{
  private StringBuffer brand;
  private StringBuffer make;
  private int compression;

  //...
  static boolean compare(StringBuffer sb1, StringBuffer sb2)
  {
    if (sb1 == sb2)
      return true;

    if (sb1 != null && sb2 != null)
    {
      int len = sb1.length();
      if (len != sb2.length())  //If lengths are not equal,
        return false;           //strings can't be either.

      int index = 0;
      while(index != len)
      {
        if (sb1.charAt(index) != sb2.charAt(index))
          return false;
        else
          index++;
      }
      return true;
    }
    return false;
  }

  public boolean equals(Object obj)
  {
    if (this == obj)
      return true;
```

```
        if (obj != null && getClass() == obj.getClass())
        {
          Golfball gb = (Golfball)obj;
          if (compare(brand, gb.brand()) &&
              compare(make, gb.make()) &&
              compression == gb.compression())
          {
            return true;
          }
        }
        return false;
      }
    }
```

What are the morals of the `equals` method story?

- To compare objects, it is the responsibility of the class to provide a correct implementation of an `equals` method.

- Before blindly calling `equals`, check to be sure the class you use implements the `equals` method.

- If it does not, determine whether the default `java.lang.Object` implementation is sufficient.

- If it is not, write your own `equals` method in a wrapper class or a subclass.

Before you write your own `equals` method, see PRAXES 11 through 15.

PRAXIS 11:   Implement the `equals` method judiciously

You should consider several issues when designing and implementing an `equals` method for a given class. First, though, you must consider when it is appropriate for a class to provide one.

An `equals` method should be provided by a class if equality of an object of that class requires more than a comparison of its object reference. In other words, a class should provide an `equals` method if two objects of that class can logically be considered the same even if they do not occupy the same space in memory.

PRAXIS 10 shows several implementations of an `equals` method for a `Golfball` class. These implementations of the `equals` method, although correct for that design and implementation, do not represent the only way to implement one.

Before writing an `equals` method, you must make an important design decision. What classes of objects do you want to be compared for equality with your class? Do you want only objects of the same class to be compared? Or, do you want objects of a derived class to be compared with objects of their base class? Next, you must decide how to implement the `equals` method to enable and enforce these semantics.

The answers to these questions directly affect the implementation of your `equals` method and the equality semantics of your class. PRAXES 12 through 15 examine these options, their ramifications, and their implementations.

PRAXIS 12:   Prefer `getClass` in `equals` method implementations

A strong argument can be made to allow only objects of the same class to be considered equal. The reasoning is that two objects cannot be equal if their classes, or types, are not the same. Allowing only objects of the same class to be considered equal is a clean and simple solution to implementing the `equals` method correctly. To do this, you use the `getClass` method in the implementation of the `equals` method. (`getClass` was used in the `equals` method implementations in PRAXIS 10.) For example:

```
class Base
{
  public boolean equals(Object obj)
  {
    if (getClass() != obj.getClass())
      return false;
    //...
  }
}
```

The `getClass` method returns the runtime class of an object. Therefore, if the objects being compared are not both of class `Base`, the `equals` method returns `false`. The following code produces the indicated results with objects of class `Base` and `Derived`:

```
class Derived extends Base
{}
//...
Base b1 = new Base();
Base b2 = new Base();
Derived d1 = new Derived();
Derived d2 = new Derived();
```

```
if (b1.equals(d1))   //Always false, classes are unequal.
if (d1.equals(b1))   //Always false, classes are unequal.
if (b1.equals(b2))   //Classes are equal, might return true if
                     //attributes are the same.
if (d1.equals(d2))   //Classes are equal, might return true if
                     //attributes are the same.
```

Because the b1 and d1 objects are of different classes, the getClass comparison always returns false. Because comparing objects of the same class passes the getClass test, whether the equals method returns true depends on whether the attributes of the classes compared are the same. Therefore, the usage of getClass does not allow an object of a derived class to be considered equal with an object of its base class. In other words, this type of comparison always results in false.

Additional guidelines should be followed, other than using the getClass method, when implementing an equals method to ensure correct and intuitive equality semantics. The implementation of an equals method differs depending on the answer to two questions:

1. What is your notion of equality? For example, two objects might be equal if all, or some, of their attributes are the same. This issue is covered shortly.

2. Does the class for which you are implementing an equals method have any base classes other than java.lang.Object? If so, do any of these base classes implement an equals method? This issue is covered in PRAXIS 13.

The answer to the first question can be illustrated by using the same Golfball class from PRAXIS 10. There, an equals method was provided for the Golfball class because objects of that type were being compared for equality. For two Golfball objects to be equal, their three attributes—brand, make, and compression—must be the same. The class, along with its equals method, is implemented like this:

```
class Golfball
{
  private String brand;
  private String make;
  private int compression;
  public Golfball (String str, String mk, int comp)
  {
    brand = str;
    make = mk;
    compression = comp;
  }
```

```
    public String brand()
    {
      return brand;
    }

    public String make()
    {
      return make;
    }

    public int compression()
    {
      return compression;
    }

    public boolean equals(Object obj)
    {
      if (this == obj)
        return true;

      if (obj != null && getClass() == obj.getClass())
      {
        Golfball gb = (Golfball)obj;  //Classes are equal, downcast.
        if (brand.equals(gb.brand()) &&  //Compare attributes.
            make.equals(gb.make()) &&
            compression == gb.compression())
        {
          return true;
        }
      }
      return false;
    }
}
```

The `equals` method first checks to see whether the two object references being compared refer to the same object. The code:

```
if (this == obj)
  return true;
```

tests whether `this` and `obj` refer to the same object. If they do, you can return `true` and not execute the rest of the method. The second test:

```
if ((obj != null) && (getClass() == obj.getClass()))
{
  //Compare attributes and return true if they are all the same
}
return false;
```

ensures you do not call `getClass` on a `null` object and the objects being compared are of the same class. If the objects being compared are of the same class, you can downcast the object to your type and perform the equality checking of the relevant attributes.

The `equals` method of class `Golfball` accurately compares two `Golfball` objects for equality based on the class designer's definition of equality. Notice that this class compares all of the attributes of the class for equality. If you decide that `compression`, although a relevant attribute of the `Golfball` class, should not be part of the equality semantics of the class, you can remove the comparison of the `compression` attribute from the `equals` method. This does not make the implementation of `equals` wrong. It simply changes the equality semantics that you are expressing through the `equals` method implementation.

In summary, an `equals` method is best implemented with `getClass`. This ensures that only like classes are ever considered equal. In addition, `equals` methods should check to see whether the objects being compared are the same object. Furthermore, an `equals` method does not need to compare all attributes of its class—only the attributes that are considered relevant to determine equality.

PRAXIS 13: **Call `super.equals` of base classes**

To ensure an `equals` method produces the correct result, it often needs to invoke the `equals` method of its base class. To illustrate, assume the `Golfball` class from PRAXIS 12 is part of a library you are using to count the number of golf balls in stock at a golf equipment warehouse. Data is read in from a database and placed in `Golfball` objects. These objects are then compared in order to generate a count. This code works fine, until you want to differentiate golf balls based on another attribute: ball construction. Because the `Golfball` class is part of a library you use, you cannot modify that code directly. Therefore, you create a subclass to add this additional attribute and provide an `equals` method to compare objects of this class. The code might look like this:

```
class MyGolfball extends Golfball
{
  public final static byte TwoPiece = 0;
  public final static byte ThreePiece = 1;
  private byte ballConstruction;
```

```
  public MyGolfball(String str, String mk,
                    int comp, byte construction)
  {
    super(str, mk, comp);
    ballConstruction = construction;
  }

  public byte construction()
  {
    return ballConstruction;
  }

  public boolean equals(Object obj)
  {
    if (this == obj)
      return true;

    if (obj != null && getClass() == obj.getClass())
    {
      MyGolfball gb = (MyGolfball)obj;  //Class equal, downcast.
      if (ballConstruction == gb.construction())
        return true;
    }
    return false;
  }
}
```

The code that counts the Golfball objects looks like this:

```
class Warehouse
{
  public static void main(String args[])
  {
    MyGolfball gb1 = new MyGolfball("BrandX", "Professional",
                                    100, MyGolfball.TwoPiece);
    MyGolfball gb2 = new MyGolfball("BrandX", "Professional",
                                    100, MyGolfball.TwoPiece);
    //...
    if (gb1.equals(gb2))
      System.out.println("Ball 1 equals Ball 2");
    else
      System.out.println("Ball 1 does not equal Ball 2");
  }
}
```

Running this code indicates that the two Golfball objects are the same. That is the correct result, but what happens when you make the Golfball objects contain different attributes?

```
MyGolfball gb1 = new MyGolfball("BrandX", "Professional",
                                90, MyGolfball.TwoPiece);
MyGolfball gb2 = new MyGolfball("BrandX", "Professional",
                                100, MyGolfball.TwoPiece);
```

Here, the `compression` attribute of the two objects differs. Calling `equals` with these unequal objects results in:

```
Ball 1 equals Ball 2
```

Clearly, this is not correct. According to the design, these two objects should not be equal. What happened?

In the `main` method of the `Warehouse` class, the code:

```
if (gb1.equals(gb2))
```

calls the `equals` method of the `MyGolfball` class because `gb1` is an object of that class. This `equals` method compares the `ballConstruction` attributes of the two `MyGolfball` objects and returns `true` because they are equal. What did not execute was the `equals` method of the base class `Golfball`. The `brand`, `make`, and `compression` attributes are stored in the base class and were not compared.

The `equals` method of the base class needs to execute in order to compare the base class attributes. After all, a `MyGolfball` object is made up of a `MyGolfball` part and a `Golfball` part. To accurately compare these objects, you need to ensure the `equals` method of both the base and derived classes are executed. This ensures the attributes of both parts of the objects are compared in order to determine equality. This is represented like this:

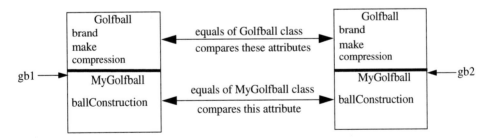

Therefore, the `equals` method for the derived class, `MyGolfball`, should be modified to invoke the `equals` method of its base class, `Golfball`:

```
public boolean equals(Object obj)
{
  if (this == obj)                                          //1
    return true;

  if (obj != null && getClass() == obj.getClass() &&        //2
      super.equals(obj))                                    //3
  {
    MyGolfball gb = (MyGolfball)obj;  //Classes equal, downcast.
    if (ballConstruction == gb.construction())  //Compare attrs.
      return true;
  }
  return false;
}
```

The equals method of MyGolfball is modified with the code at //3. This calls the equals method of the base class, Golfball, to compare its attributes. If the base class attributes (brand, make, and compression) are the same, the code compares the derived class attribute (ballConstruction). Running this code with the equal and unequal objects produces the correct results.

A shortcut is available that you might be able to take with the implementation of the equals method of the derived class. In the previous example, the code at //1 and //2 can be removed. Because the equals method of the base class is called with super.equals and performs the identical checks, using both is redundant. The equals method implemented with this shortcut looks like this:

```
public boolean equals(Object obj)
{
  if (super.equals(obj))
  {
    MyGolfball gb = (MyGolfball)obj;  //Classes equal, downcast.
    if (ballConstruction == gb.construction())
      return true;
  }
  return false;
}
```

Using this shortcut, however, requires you to have access to the source code of the base class in order to ensure the proper checking is done there. In addition, this shortcut compels you to risk future code breakage as a result of class hierarchy modifications. For example, if a derived class that uses this shortcut is modified to become a base class, its equals method must be updated to add the checks back in. Use this shortcut only if you find that removing it gives you enough of a performance boost to warrant the associated risks.

What if there is another class between `Golfball` and `MyGolfball`? For example:

```
class Golfball
{
  public boolean equals(Object obj){}
  //As before...
}
class NewGolfball extends Golfball
{
  //Doesn't provide an equals method
}
class MyGolfball extends NewGolfball
{
  public boolean equals(Object obj){}
  //As before...
}
```

Because the `equals` method of `MyGolfball` calls `super.equals`, the code works properly and produces the correct result. When writing an `equals` method for a derived class, you must check all base classes other than `java.lang.Object` for an `equals` method implementation. If any has one, then you must call `super.equals`.

You check all base classes other than `java.lang.Object` because of the `equals` method implementation in `java.lang.Object`. This method simply compares two object references for equality. What you are trying to accomplish is to compare specific attributes of the classes. If a base class has an `equals` method, it is comparing specific attributes of that class. If you derive from that class, you must call its `equals` method to compare its attributes. Put another way, call `super.equals` if any base class other than `java.lang.Object` implements an `equals` method.

PRAXIS 14: Consider carefully `instanceof` in `equals` method implementations

PRAXIS 12 shows how using `getClass` in an `equals` method implementation allows only objects of the same class to be considered equal. However, what if you want derived class objects to equal their base class objects?

For example, consider a class library that provides a class that represents a car. This class provides some attributes about the car and some methods for manipulating the car. The class might look like this:

```
class Car
{
  private String make;
  private int year;
  public void drive()
  {
    //Code to drive the car...
  }
  public boolean equals(Object obj)
  {
    //Compare make and year for equality...
  }
  //...
}
```

Assume you create objects of class Car and use them in your application. In addition, you often compare different Car objects for equality. Two Car objects are equal if their make and year are the same. You then want to change the driving behavior of some of your cars. Assuming you cannot change the source code of the Car class, you derive your own class, MyCar:

```
class MyCar extends Car
{
  public void drive()
  {
    //Code to drive the car differently than base class, Car
  }
}
```

Notice that no attributes are added to the MyCar class. Only behavior is added with the overridden drive method. When creating Car objects, you create both Car objects and MyCar objects. Remember, you are only changing the drive behavior of some of your cars. Therefore, you will be comparing MyCar objects to Car objects for equality. You still want your equality comparison to work because the relevant attributes to be compared are in the base class Car, not in the derived class MyCar.

Given this scenario, you can conclude that it is valid to compare objects of a derived class with objects of its base class. To perform this type of comparison, two conditions must exist:

1. The base class implements an equals method using instanceof, not get-Class.

2. The derived class does not implement an equals method.

The rationale for this is as follows:

- To support comparison between derived class objects and base class objects, the equals method in the base class must not use getClass. When getClass is used in an equals method for a given class, all objects derived from this class are considered unequal to objects of their base class. Instead, if a class uses instanceof, objects derived from it can be considered equal to objects of their base class.

- If a derived class does not implement an equals method, then you can presume it did not add any attributes to be considered in an expression of equality. Therefore, you can rely on the base class implementation of the equals method to compare the relevant attributes of the base classes.

- If a derived class does implement an equals method, then you can assume it has additional attributes that must be compared for equality. These attributes would be compared with other instances of the derived class or objects derived from it. These objects should not be compared with instances of superclass objects.

For example, consider the following class definitions and object declarations:

```
class Base
{
  public boolean equals(Object obj)
  {
    if (obj instanceof Base)
    //...
  }
}

class Derived extends Base
{}

//...

Base b = new Base();
Derived d = new Derived();
if (d.equals(b))  //Potentially true if Base attributes are equal
if (b.equals(d))  //Potentially true if Base attributes are equal
//...
```

This situation is represented like this:

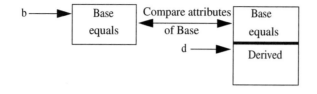

Because class `Base` implements an `equals` method with `instanceof` and the derived class does not, comparing objects of class `Derived` with objects of class `Base` potentially returns `true`. In addition, this comparison is symmetrical. For example:

```
b.equals(d) == d.equals(b)
```

However, if the `equals` method in class `Base` is implemented with `getClass`, this comparison always returns `false`. The `getClass` method would return different values for b and d. (For more on `getClass`, see PRAXIS 12.)

What if both the base and derived class implement an `equals` method? As discussed previously, you want equality comparisons of this type to return `false`. The existence of an `equals` method in a derived class indicates it has additional attributes not contained in its base class. For example, consider the following base and derived classes:

```
class Base
{
  private int attributeOfBase;
  public boolean equals(Object obj)
  {
    if (obj instanceof Base)
      //...
  }
}

class Derived extends Base
{
  private int attributeOfDerived;
  public boolean equals(Object obj)
  {
    if (obj instanceof Derived)
    //...
  }
}
```

The code, d.equals(b), is always false because the equals method of class Derived contains the code:

```
if (obj instanceof Derived)
```

In this case, obj is of type Base and Base is not an instance of Derived. This produces the desired result. However, some libraries contain sloppily written code that attempts to shortcut the instanceof check. The equals method of the derived class is written to simply call super.equals(obj) and allow the instanceof test to be performed in the base class. Coding such a shortcut produces code that looks and behaves as follows:

```
class Base
{
  public boolean equals(Object obj)
  {
    if (obj instanceof Base)                               //1
      //...
  }
}

class Derived extends Base
{
  public boolean equals(Object obj)
  {
    if (super.equals(obj))  //Superclass performs instanceof check
    //...
  }
}
```

With this design, d.equals(b) is now potentially true and symmetry is lost. This happens because the equals method of the derived class is invoked with an object of type Base. Because the instanceof check has been replaced with a call to super.equals, the code executes the equals method of class Base. The test at //1 is now true because an object of class Base is an instance of class Base. This code now allows an invalid comparison. Remember, an object of a derived class that implements an equals method should not return true when it is compared to its base class for equality. Avoid this shortcut to eliminate this problem.

You still, however, need to call super.equals when a base class other than java.lang.Object has an equals method. This is covered in detail in PRAXIS 13. The point to remember is to still code the instanceof check, then call super.equals as needed.

Another problem with comparing objects of derived classes with objects of base classes is that no way exists to preserve symmetry in your comparisons if both classes implement an equals method with instanceof. For example, consider the previous case in which both the base and derived classes implement an equals method with an instanceof check. Remember, both classes contain an equals method because both have attributes that can be compared for equality with other derived objects. You have implemented both equals methods to use the instanceof check in order to ensure comparisons between derived and base objects always return false. For example:

```
class Base
{
  public boolean equals(Object obj)
  {
    if (obj instanceof Base)
      //...
  }
}

class Derived extends Base
{
  public boolean equals(Object obj)
  {
    if (obj instanceof Derived)
    //...
  }
}

Base b = new Base();
Derived d = new Derived();
```

Executing this code:

```
 if (d.equals(b))
```

always returns false. This is because the equals method of the derived class is called with an object of type Base. An object of type Base is not an instance of Derived, so the instanceof check results in false being returned.

However, what happens if you code your equality comparison like this?

```
 if (b.equals(d))
```

In this case, the equals method of class Base is invoked, passing an object of type Derived. The instanceof check succeeds because an object of class Derived is an instance of class `Base`. Therefore, if the attributes of the base classes are equal, you get the following results:

```
if (d.equals(b))  //Always false
if (b.equals(d))  //Always true
```

This behavior is non-intuitive and therefore not desirable for your classes. In addition, there is no solution to this problem. To compare derived class objects with base class objects, you must accept the potential for this problem. You might think you can be careful and code your tests with the most derived class object first to avoid this. This notion has several problems:

- You must remember to code your tests this way.

- If you are providing classes for use by others, they must also follow this rule.

- Often, you are accessing objects through their base class references. For example, retrieving a derived class object from a `Vector` returns an object reference with type `java.lang.Object`. Without performing additional costly checking, you do not know which is the derived class.

Therefore, you have two choices to implement an `equals` method. You can use `getClass` in your `equals` methods and preserve symmetry in all cases (see PRAXIS 12). For example,

```
x.equals(y) == y.equals(x)
```

However, remember that using `getClass` always results in `false` when objects of derived classes are compared to objects of base classes. Alternatively, you can use `instanceof` in your `equals` methods—this allows objects of derived classes to be considered equal to objects of their base classes.

If you choose to use `instanceof`, the following summarizes the three situations regarding the `equals` methods of derived classes that are implemented with `instanceof`:

1. The base class implements an `equals` method and the derived class does not.

    Assuming the `equals` method of the base class uses `instanceof`, you can compare objects of the derived class with objects of the base class. In addition, comparisons between base and derived objects are symmetrical.

2. The base and derived classes both implement an `equals` method.

   If the `equals` method of both classes use `instanceof`, you want `false` returned when comparing objects of the derived class with objects of the base class. `false` is returned when the `equals` method of the derived class is called because objects of class `Base` are not instances of class `Derived`. However, `true` can be returned if the `equals` method of the base class is called. The `equals` method called depends on the position of the object reference variables in the `equals` method invocation.

3. The base class does not implement an `equals` method, but the derived class does.

   `false` is returned when the `equals` method of the derived class is called because objects of class `Base` are not instances of class `Derived`. `false` also is returned when the `equals` method of the base class is called, although for a different reason. Because the base class does not implement an `equals` method, the `equals` method of `java.lang.Object` is invoked and compares the two object references for equality (see PRAXIS 10).

Unfortunately, comparisons between base and derived objects complicate the implementation of the `equals` method and introduces problems that you might not find acceptable.

A quick glance through the source code of the Java libraries shows the use of `instanceof` in `equals` method implementations is common. You also find the use of `getClass`. The Java libraries are not consistent in how they implement the `equals` methods of their classes, thereby making consistent equality comparisons difficult.

This raises yet another problem with the use of `instanceof` in an `equals` method. If you are using a class library, such as the Java libraries or a third-party library, you need to know how the classes you use implement their `equals` methods. Do they use `getClass` or `instanceof`? If they use `instanceof`, do they incorrectly call `super.equals` in a derived class and rely on the base class to implement the `instanceof` check?

Without the source code with which to examine the classes, you must write test code to determine how the `equals` methods are implemented. Knowing how they are implemented alerts you to potential problems that you or users of your code might encounter.

Furthermore, if you are implementing an `equals` method for a derived class, and its base class contains an `equals` method implemented with `instanceof`, how should you implement the `equals` method of the derived class? The best approach is to use `getClass`.

By using `getClass`, you establish that only objects of your derived class can be considered equal. You still need to call `super.equals` to compare your base class attributes, but the existence of `instanceof` in the base class does not cause these comparisons to fail. The class still exhibits the symmetry problems though, due to the use of `instanceof` in the base class. For example:

```
class Base
{
  public boolean equals(Object obj)
  {
    if (obj instanceof Base)
    //...
  }
}

class Derived extends Base
{
  public boolean equals(Object obj)
  {
    if (obj != null && getClass() == obj.getClass() &&
        super.equals(obj))
    //...
  }
}

Base b = new Base();
Derived d = new Derived();
if (d.equals(b))  //Always false
if (b.equals(d))  //Potentially true
```

There are valid reasons for wanting to support equality comparisons between base and derived class objects. However, given all of the problems with the use of `instanceof`, the recommended way to implement an `equals` method is to use `getClass` (see PRAXIS 12). This allows only objects of the same class to be considered equal and alleviates all of the problems with `instanceof`.

PRAXIS 15: **Follow these rules when implementing an equals method**

The preceding four PRAXES show that writing an equals method is not as straightforward as you might have thought. You must understand various issues so that your implementation of an equals method produces the correct result.

Regardless of whether you choose to implement an equals method with getClass or instanceof, the following rules apply to all equals method implementations:

- Provide an equals method for a class when two objects of that class can logically be considered the same even if they do not occupy the same space in memory.

- Check for comparison to this (see PRAXIS 12).

- Compare all relevant attributes of the class to determine equality (see PRAXIS 12).

- Call super.equals if any base class other than java.lang.Object implements an equals method (see PRAXIS 13).

The following are the issues to be considered when determining whether you implement the equals method with getClass or instanceof:

- Generally use getClass to allow only objects of the same class to be considered equal (see PRAXIS 12).

- Use instanceof only if you must compare objects of derived classes with objects of base classes and you understand the problems and complications that doing this yields (see PRAXIS 14).

- If you use instanceof, understand that your comparisons will not exhibit symmetric equality if both the derived class and base class implement an equals method (see PRAXIS 14).

Exception Handling

EXCEPTION handling is a powerful and useful feature of the Java language. With this power comes a degree of complexity that must be overcome in order to effectively utilize exception handling in Java programs. Java introduces new concepts to previous exception handling models that make exceptions both easier and more difficult to use properly.

Exception handling is not the silver bullet it is sometimes made out to be. It does not solve all of your error handling problems. In fact, it introduces new problems unless you understand how to properly use exceptions. Too often with exception handling, programmers believe that mastering a few new keywords solves their error handling problems. In fact, exception handling simply represents a different avenue to deal with errors. While it is a step forward with regard to traditional error handling techniques, failure to fully understand it leads to the creation of additional faults in your error handling code.

Writing fault-tolerant, mission-critical software requires an effective and stalwart error handling and recovery strategy. Implementing this is difficult and time consuming. Used properly, the information in this section minimizes the difficulty and the amount of time spent to generate robust software. However, if you put off the decision to consider these issues until the end of the development cycle you will pay a heavy price.

PRAXIS 16 reviews some important program flow mechanics so you can fully comprehend the other material in this section.

PRAXIS 16: **Know the mechanics of exception control flow**

To write robust Java code that deals with error conditions properly, you must have a firm grasp of the mechanics involved. One element that makes exceptions difficult to deal with is that they behave like goto statements. Java does not provide a goto statement in the language, but exception handling employs a similar technique. When an exception is generated, control is immediately transferred to one of three places:

- `catch` block

- `finally` block

- the calling method

This is the "goto" behavior of exceptions. Knowing this is important for several reasons. The most important is covered in PRAXIS 27, where the criticality of object state is discussed. Another reason is your code can jump from one location to another. Depending on the structure of the code, this can lead to complicated logic, thereby making the code difficult to debug (see PRAXIS 18). Consider the following code:

```java
class ExceptionTest {
  public static void main (String args[])
  {
    System.out.println("Entering main()");
    ExceptionTest et = new ExceptionTest();
    try {
      System.out.println("Calling m1()");
      et.m1();
      System.out.println("Returning from call to m1()");      //1
    }
    catch (Exception e) {
      System.out.println("Caught IOException in main()");
    }
    System.out.println("Exiting main()");
  }

  public void m1() throws IOException
  {
    System.out.println("Entering m1()");
    Button b1 = new Button();
    try {
      System.out.println("Calling m2()");
      m2();
      System.out.println("Returning from call to m2()");
      System.out.println("Calling m3()");
```

```
      m3(true);
      System.out.println("Returning from call to m3()");        //2
    }
    catch (IOException e) {
      System.out.println("Caught IOException in " +
                         "m1()...rethrowing");
      throw e;                                                   //3
    }
    finally {
      System.out.println("In finally for m1()");
    }
    System.out.println("Exiting m1()");                          //4
  }

  public void m2()
  {
    System.out.println("Entering m2()");
    try {
      Vector v = new Vector(5);
    }
    catch (IllegalArgumentException iae) {
      System.out.println("Caught " +
        "IllegalArgumentException in m2()");                     //5
    }
    finally {
      System.out.println("In finally for m2()");
    }
    System.out.println("Exiting m2()");
  }

  public void m3(boolean genExc) throws IOException
  {
    System.out.println("Entering m3()");
    try {
      Button b3 = new Button();
      if (genExc)
        throw new IOException();
    }
    finally {
      System.out.println("In finally for m3()");
    }
    System.out.println("Exiting m3()");                          //6
  }
}
```

The output from this code is:

```
Entering main()
Calling m1()
Entering m1()
```

```
Calling m2()
Entering m2()
In finally for m2()
Exiting m2()
Returning from call to m2()
Calling m3()
Entering m3()
In finally for m3()
Caught IOException in m1()...rethrowing
In finally for m1()
Caught IOException in main()
Exiting main()
```

Here is a detailed trace of the code. When this code is invoked, it prints a message, enters a try block, and prints another message. Method m1 is then called. When method m1 is entered, a message is printed, a try block is entered, and another message is printed. Method m2 is then called.

When method m2 is entered, a message is printed and then a try block is entered. The code in this try block executes without throwing an exception. Therefore, the catch block is skipped and control transfers to the finally block of method m2. A message is printed in the finally block, and another message is printed before this method exits. Method m2 returns to where it was called from in method m1, prints two messages, and then calls method m3.

When method m3 is entered, a message is printed and then a try block is entered. An exception is then thrown from the try block. Before this method exits, the finally block for method m3 is executed and a message is printed. Control then transfers to the catch block of the calling method m1. This catch block prints a message and rethrows the exception. Before leaving method m1, its finally block is executed and a message is printed before it returns to the calling method, main.

Method main enters its catch block and prints a message. Because the exception is handled there and not rethrown, control proceeds after this catch block and a message is printed at the bottom of method main. The program then terminates.

This trace shows that when an exception is thrown, execution of the corresponding code is immediately stopped and control is transferred elsewhere. Notice that the lines at //1, //2, //4, //5, and //6 are not in the output.

The code at //1 and //2 is not executed because an exception is generated on the previous line that results in the direct transfer of control to the catch block of the method. The code at //4 and //6 is not executed because after the exception is thrown and not caught, control is transferred out of the method immediately after the execution of the `finally` block. (If the exception is not rethrown at //3, the code at //4 will be executed.) The code at //5 is not executed because the `catch` block that contains this code is never invoked, since an exception is not thrown from the corresponding `try` block.

This also shows that when an exception is thrown from a `try` block, the following happens:

- If there are `catch` and `finally` blocks, control is transferred to the `catch` block and then to the `finally` block.

- If there is no `catch` block, control is transferred to the `finally` block.

Because Java supports garbage collection, you do not have to worry about cleaning up object memory. This applies to the `Button` and `Vector` objects created in the previous example. All objects created in a method are unreferenced automatically if the method completes normally or exits abruptly due to an exception. Therefore, you do not have to manually unreference these object references (see PRAXIS 7). You do, however, have to explicitly clean up non-memory resources (see PRAXES 21 and 67).

Depending on your perspective, another aspect of exception handling is viewed as either good news or bad: You cannot easily ignore an exception. If you think that ignoring an exception is a good idea or are wondering what happens if you do, see PRAXIS 17.

Understanding the mechanics of exception handling control flow is imperative to writing robust code. Failure to understand exactly what is happening as exceptions are generated leads to programs that behave incorrectly and are difficult to extend and maintain.

PRAXIS 17:   **Never ignore an exception**

When an exception is generated, what happens if you do not catch it? In Java, if an exception is generated and not caught, the thread on which the exception occurred terminates. Therefore, you must deal with the exceptions generated in your code.

When an exception is generated in Java, what can you do?

1. Catch the exception and handle it so that it does not propagate further.

2. Catch the exception and rethrow it so that it propagates to the calling method.

3. Catch the exception and throw a new one to the calling method.

4. Do not catch the exception and let it propagate to the calling method.

For checked exceptions, options 2, 3, and 4 require you to add the exception to the throws clause of your method (see PRAXES 19 and 20). Option 1 stops the exception from propagating further. When using option 3, be sure the new exception thrown contains the relevant information from the original exception. This ensures important information is not lost (see PRAXIS 18).

Often, option 1 is used, although in an ill-advised fashion, to ignore the exception. For example, the code catches the exception, but does not do anything with it, as follows:

```java
public void m1()
{
  //...
  try {
    //Code that could throw a FileNotFoundException
  }
  catch (FileNotFoundException fnfe)
  {} //The exception stops here
  //...Rest of code in method
}
```

This code ignores the exception. If the exception occurs, it is caught and not rethrown. Notice that the exception is not handled and the code after the catch block resumes execution as if nothing happened. Nothing was done with it other than it was "eaten." "Eating" an exception requires more work than does simply ignoring a return code because you have to place the try/catch block around the code that could throw the exception. (There is a situation, shown in PRAXIS 54, where you might purposefully ignore an exception.)

If you write code like this or work with someone who does, be aware that this is unwise because there is no record that the exception occurred. Therefore, your code tries to continue as if nothing happened. The danger is that your code will probably fail later, resulting in a much more difficult situation to debug. If you do not know what to do with an exception at the early stages of development, then at a minimum do something like the following:

```
public void m1()
{
  //...
  try {
    //Code that could throw a FileNotFoundException
  }
  catch (FileNotFoundException fnfe)
  {
    System.out.println(fnfe + " caught in method m1");
    LogException(fnfe);
  }
}
```

This at least gives you some output and a log file to indicate that an exception occurred and you have a problem in your code. This technique also serves as a reminder that exceptions are being generated without proper recovery mechanisms in place. You can then go to the code, which is represented by the log file entries, and insert proper exception handling code. (Note, the LogException method is provided by you and simply writes exception information to a file.)

The disadvantage of this approach is the log file includes only the exceptions that occurred as a result of your tests. Exceptions that did not occur are not included. Therefore, addressing everything in the log file after a given test does not necessarily mean that you have fully cleaned up your code. It only indicates that you have a list of exceptions that occurred during a given test.

To find exceptions that did not occur during the test, you must search your source code for all occurrences of LogException or some other type of tag you insert as a comment. This is the only way to ensure that you have not left in a simple println statement where proper exception handling code should be.

Another useful approach is to use the printStackTrace method. This method provides the exception thrown and a stack trace to where the exception originated to the standard error stream. The modified code with this technique looks like this:

```
public void m1()
{
  //...
  try {
    //Code that could throw a FileNotFoundException
  }
```

```
    catch (FileNotFoundException fnfe)
    {
      System.out.println(fnfe + " caught in method m1");
      fnfe.printStackTrace();
    }
}
```

Remember when using this technique to redirect the standard error stream output to a file. This enables the file to be parsed to determine if any exceptions were generated. On Windows and UNIX, this is done by directing standard error and standard output to the same file as follows:

```
java Test > out.dat 2>&1
```

The best approach, however, is not to put off the dirty work of exception and error handling, but rather to deal with it as they arise.

PRAXIS 18: **Never hide an exception**

Exceptions are hidden when one is thrown from a catch or finally block during the processing of a previously thrown exception. Only the last exception generated is propagated to the calling method. If you are interested only in the fact that a method failed due to one or more exceptions, you might not care if a previously thrown exception is hidden. However, you want to avoid hiding exceptions when you want to know the original cause of a method's failure.

Often during catch or finally block processing, you call methods that can throw exceptions. How do you handle this so that previously thrown exceptions are not hidden? You need a mechanism to transfer *all* generated exceptions of a method to the calling method. Here is an example of the problem:

```
class Hidden
{
  public static void main (String args[])
  {
    Hidden h = new Hidden();
    try {
      h.foo();
    }
    catch (Exception e) {
      System.out.println("In main, caught exception: " +
                          e.getMessage());
    }
  }
```

```
    public void foo() throws Exception
    {
      try {
        throw new Exception("First Exception");              //1
      }
      catch (Exception e) {
        throw new Exception("Second Exception");             //2
      }
      finally {
        throw new Exception("Third Exception");              //3
      }
    }
  }
```

Running this code produces the following output:

```
    In main, caught exception: Third Exception
```

This code calls method foo from main and prints the exception thrown from foo. The output shows that the exception thrown from foo is the exception generated in the finally block at //3. What happened to the exceptions generated in the try and the catch at //1 and //2?

The exception thrown at //1 is hidden by the exception thrown at //2. The exception thrown at //2 is hidden by the exception thrown at //3. Because the exception thrown at //3 is the last one thrown from the method, it is the exception that is ultimately generated by the method; the others are lost.

You might think that this situation does not arise in typical Java code. Actually, it is common, as the following example illustrates:

```
    import java.io.*;
    class Hidden
    {
      public static void main(String args[])
      {
        Hidden h = new Hidden();
        try {
          h.readFile();
        }
        catch (FileNotFoundException fne) {
          //...
        }
        catch (IOException ioe) {
          //...
        }
      }
```

```
public void readFile() throws FileNotFoundException,
                                IOException
{
  BufferedReader br1 = null;
  BufferedReader br2 = null;
  FileReader fr = null;

  try {
    fr = new FileReader("data1.fil");                      //1
    br1 = new BufferedReader(fr);
    int i = br1.read();                                    //2
    //Other code...
    fr = new FileReader("data2.fil");                      //3
    br2 = new BufferedReader(fr);
    i = br2.read();                                        //4
    //Other code...
  }
  finally {
    if (br1 != null)
      br1.close();                                         //5
    if (br2 != null)
      br2.close();                                         //6
  }
}
}
```

This example has a readFile method that reads data from a file. It can throw two different types of exceptions: A FileNotFoundException, which can be generated at //1 and //3, and an IOException, which can be generated from //2, //4, //5, or //6. This method also uses a finally block to close the BufferedReader object when it exits. These calls are placed in a finally block to ensure they are always executed (see PRAXES 16 and 21). The close methods in the finally block can also generate an IOException and are the source of the problem.

This code can hide exceptions under certain situations. When a FileNotFound-Exception is generated at //3, control transfers to the finally block, where br1 is closed. What happens if the br1.close call results in an IOException? If this occurs, the IOException is returned to the calling method but the FileNot-FoundException is not. The calling method will not know that the method originally failed due to a file not being found.

If an exception occurs and control is transferred to a catch or a finally block, which then generates another exception, what should you do? Remember that exceptions can be generated from anywhere and are still active during catch and finally blocks. In addition, try, catch, and finally blocks can be arbitrarily nested within one another.

One solution to this problem is to save a list of all exceptions generated. Then throw an exception that holds a reference to this list. In this way, the receiver of the new exception has information about all exceptions and critical error information is not lost.

The previous code is modified as follows to contain a new class to contain all of the exceptions that are generated from the `readFile` method. The `readFile` method adds all generated exceptions to a `Vector` and stores a reference to this `Vector` in a `ReadFileExceptions` object, which is thrown to the calling method. The modified code looks like this:

```
import java.io.*;
import java.util.Vector;

class ReadFileExceptions extends Exception
{
  private Vector excVector;
  public ReadFileExceptions(Vector v)
  {
    excVector = v;
  }
  public Vector exceptionVector()
  {
    return excVector;
  }
  //...
}

class NotHidden
{
  public static void main(String args[])
  {
    NotHidden nh = new NotHidden();
    try {
      nh.readFile();
    }
    catch (ReadFileExceptions rfe) {
      //...
    }
  }

  public void readFile() throws ReadFileExceptions
  {
    BufferedReader br1 = null;
    BufferedReader br2 = null;
    FileReader fr = null;
    Vector excVec = new Vector(2);  //Vector to store exceptions
```

```
        try {
          fr = new FileReader("data1.fil");
          br1 = new BufferedReader(fr);
          int i = br1.read();
          //Other code...
          fr = new FileReader("data2.fil");
          br2 = new BufferedReader(fr);
          i = br2.read();
          //Other code...
        }
        catch (FileNotFoundException fnfe) {
          excVec.add(fnfe);   //Add exception to Vector
        }
        catch (IOException ioe){
          excVec.add(ioe);   //Add exception to Vector
        }
        finally {
          if (br1 != null)
          {
            try {
              br1.close();
            }
            catch (IOException e) {
              excVec.add(e);   //Add exception to Vector
            }
          }
          if (br2 != null)
          {
            try {
              br2.close();
            }
            catch (IOException e) {
              excVec.add(e);   //Add exception to Vector
            }
          }
          if (excVec.size() != 0)
            throw new ReadFileExceptions(excVec);//Pass all exceptions
        }                                        //to caller.
      }
    }
```

In this code, the readFile method creates a Vector to store exceptions. Any exceptions generated are added to this Vector. Before the method exits, the Vector is checked to see if anything has been added to it. If so, the ReadFileExceptions object is created with the Vector of exceptions that have occurred in the method. Alternatively, you can create the Vector only if an exception occurs. This eliminates the overhead incurred to create the Vector and then not use it. The overhead of object creation and the cost of unused objects are covered in detail in PRAXES 32 and 33, respectively.

Failure to accommodate this problem has negative consequences, primarily that the original exception is lost and the code processing the last exception thrown does not know about the previous exceptions thrown. This is harmful when the code is attempting to recover from the exception and does not know that other errors have occurred.

This code shows that `try`, `catch`, and `finally` blocks can be arbitrarily nested. In addition, only one exception propagates from a `try`, `catch`, or `finally` block even though many might be thrown from within them. Remember that the last exception thrown is the only exception received by the caller—the others are hidden and thus lost. Hiding exceptions is not desirable if the calling code needs to know the original reason for a failure.

PRAXIS 19: Consider the drawback to the throws clause

The `throws` clause is a mechanism used to list all of the checked exceptions that can propagate from a method. The compiler ensures that you catch checked exceptions in a method or declare them in the `throws` clause of the method. The `throws` clause alerts all callers of your method to the exceptions that it generates. It is a useful language feature and provides valuable information to users of methods (see PRAXIS 20). There is a side effect to this feature, however, that you should consider as you design your code.

What happens when you are well into your coding effort of a large project and you add a checked exception to a low-level worker method? For the purposes of this discussion, a worker method is one that performs a common task for many other methods and is called from many places in your code. Typical systems have many such methods. If this situation arises, you have two choices.

1. Catch the exception in this method and handle it there.

2. Throw the exception from the worker method and allow the caller to handle it.

Depending on the design of your system, the first option might not be viable because the worker method might not have the means to resolve the exception itself. You might have no other choice but to choose the second option and throw this exception. This might not be as easy as it sounds.

Adding an exception to a throws clause of a method affects *every* method that calls it—all methods that call this worker method must change. They also have the same two choices regarding what to do as previously listed. If they decide to handle the exception, the exception does not propagate any further. However, what if some of these methods do not have the means of handling the exception? They, too, must rely on the second option and add the exception to their throws clause. After making this change, you can attempt to recompile your code. When the compiler is done spitting out error messages, you might realize what you are up against. Now, all methods that call all of the methods you just changed have the same two choices. The process continues all the way back to main, assuming no intervening method handles the exception.

To minimize the chances of encountering this problem, do not add exception handling at the end of the development cycle. Design in your error handling strategy from the beginning. If you are confronted with this situation, even with careful planning, you now know the ramifications. The throws clause is a useful and beneficial language feature, but it can also be painful to use if you are not careful.

PRAXIS 20: **Be specific and comprehensive with the throws clause**

The throws clause is provided to alert callers of a method to the checked exceptions it might generate. Given this, consider the following code that declares three types of exceptions and a method that throws all three types:

```
class Exception1 extends Exception
{}
class Exception2 extends Exception1
{}
class Exception3 extends Exception2
{}
class Lazy
{
  public void foo(int i) throws Exception1
  {
    if (i==1)
      throw new Exception1();
    if (i==2)
      throw new Exception2();
    if (i==3)
      throw new Exception3();
  }
}
```

Method foo declares a throws clause with one exception type listed. However, the method throws three different exceptions. Does this code compile cleanly? Should you write code like this?

This code is completely legal and compiles cleanly without the compiler issuing a warning. Nevertheless, writing code like this has its drawbacks. Method foo throws three exceptions, all of which are of type Exception1. Exception2 and Exception3 are derived Exception1 types. Therefore, the compile is clean because the throws clause is satisfied. The throws clause alerts callers that an exception of type Exception1 could be generated by this method. A better way to write the throws clause for method foo is as follows:

```
public void foo(int i) throws Exception1, Exception2, Exception3
```

This throws clause explicitly lists all exceptions that are generated by the method. Consider the first method foo:

```
public void foo(int i) throws Exception1
```

This throws clause informs the caller of method foo that it could generate an exception of the class Exception1. This is true, but in reality this method could also generate an exception of the class Exception2 and Exception3. The caller of the method knows only about Exception1. The only way for the caller to know about the derived exceptions this method generates is by examining the source code. This is impractical and often impossible. Therefore, when the code that calls foo is written, it looks like this:

```
//...
try {
  Lazy l = new Lazy();
  l.foo(1);
  //...
}
catch (Exception1 exc)
{
  //Handle it...
}
```

When the catch block executes as a result of an exception being thrown, you might be processing an exception of the class Exception1, Exception2, or Exception3. If you had access to the source code, you could check which exception type was thrown through the instanceof method. However, using instanceof is cumbersome. Furthermore, assuming you had access to the source, how would you know to check it? If you do not have the source, you are stuck with dealing with the least derived exception class and the hope that it has encapsulated the error information provided by the derived exception.

When specifying the throws clause, fill it in completely. Although the compiler does not enforce this being done, it is good programming practice to list all exceptions that are thrown from a method in its throws clause. Regardless of the fact that these exceptions all derive from one another, their occurrences could signify vastly different error conditions. Being verbose in your throws clause requires a bit more typing, but it saves the caller of your method time and frustration trying to figure out exactly which exceptions the method potentially generates.

All of this discussion of the throws clause brings up an interesting question. When you override a method, which exception types are you allowed to throw from the overridden method, and which do you include in its throws clause? Suppose you have the following code:

```java
import java.io.*;

class Base
{
  public void foo() throws FileNotFoundException
  {
    //...
    throw new FileNotFoundException();
  }
}

class OverrideTest extends Base
{
  public void foo() throws IOException
  {
    throw new IOException();
  }
}
```

Compiling this code results in the following output:

```
OverrideTest.java:14: The method void foo() declared in class
OverrideTest cannot override the method of the same signature
declared in class Base.  Their throws clauses are incompatible.
  public void foo() throws IOException
             ^
1 error
```

This error tells you a method that throws an exception, which also overrides its superclass method, is restricted in the exceptions thrown by the superclass method. Overridden methods can throw only exceptions of the same type as the superclass method or specializations of those types. Therefore, from method foo in class OverrideTest, you can:

- not throw any exceptions,
- throw a FileNotFoundException, or
- throw an exception derived from FileNotFoundException.

Thus, you are restricted on what you can do in your override methods. For example, if you override a method that does not throw any exceptions and add code to your override method that does, you must catch the exception in your override and handle it there. You are unable to propagate the exception out of that method.

PRAXIS 21: Use finally to avoid resource leaks

The finally keyword is the best addition to the Java exception handling model over other language's models. The finally construct enables code to execute whether or not an exception occurred (see PRAXIS 16). Using finally is good to maintain the internal state of an object and to clean up non-memory resources. Without finally, your code is more convoluted. For example, the following is how you must write code to free non-memory resources without the benefit of finally:

```java
import java.net.*;
import java.io.*;

class WithoutFinally
{
  public void foo() throws IOException
  {
    //Create a socket on any free port
    ServerSocket ss = new ServerSocket(0);
    try {
      Socket socket = ss.accept();
      //Other code here...
    }
    catch (IOException e) {
      ss.close();                                        //1
      throw e;
    }
```

```
      //...
      ss.close();                                              //2
    }
  }
```

This code creates a socket and calls the `accept` method. You must close the socket before exiting the method in order to avoid a resource leak. To do this, you call `close` as the last statement of the method at //2. What happens, however, if an exception occurs in the `try` block? In this case, the `close` call at //2 is not reached. Therefore, you must catch the exception and put in another call to `close` at //1 prior to rethrowing the exception. This ensures the socket is closed prior to exiting the method.

Writing code in this manner is bothersome and prone to error, yet necessary without the existence of `finally`. Unfortunately, in languages without a `finally` mechanism, programmers might forget to structure their code in this manner, leading to resource leaks. The `finally` clause in Java solves this problem. With `finally`, the previous code is rewritten as follows:

```
import java.net.*;
import java.io.*;

class WithFinally
{
  public void foo2() throws IOException
  {
    //Create a socket on any free port
    ServerSocket ss = new ServerSocket(0);
    try {
      Socket socket = ss.accept();
      //Other code here...
    }
    finally {
      ss.close();
    }
  }
}
```

A `finally` block ensures the `close` method is executed whether or not an exception is thrown from within the `try` block. Therefore, the `close` method is guaranteed to be called before the method exits. You are then sure the socket is closed and you have not leaked a resource. There is no longer any need to have a `catch` block in this method. The `catch` block in the first example was provided only to close the socket that is now closed with `finally`. If you did provide a catch block, the code in the finally block executes after the catch block finishes (see PRAXIS 16).

The finally block must be used in conjunction with a try or try/catch block. In addition, there is no way to exit a try block without executing its finally block. If the finally block exists, it always executes.[1]

PRAXIS 22: **Do not return from a try block**

The try/finally block is straightforward but has some behavior that catches even the knowledgeable programmer off guard. If a finally block exists, it is always executed.[1] A finally block is entered when code within a try block leaves the try block. Code leaves a try block when any of the following occurs:

- An exception is thrown.

- The try block finishes normally.

- A return, break, or continue statement is executed within a try block, thereby causing execution to leave the try block.

Look at the ramifications of this by considering the following code:

```
class FinallyTest
{
  public int method1()
  {
    try {
      return 2;
    }
    catch(Exception e) {return 3;}
  }

  public int method2()
  {
    try {
      return 3;                              //1
    }
    finally {                                //2
      return 4;
```

[1.] This statement is true for all intents and purposes. There is a way to exit a try block without executing the finally block. If the code executes a System.exit(0); from within a try block, the application terminates without the finally executing. On the other hand, if you unplug the machine during a try block, the finally will not execute either.

```
        }
    }

    public static void main(String args[])
    {
      FinallyTest ft = new FinallyTest();
      System.out.println("method1 returns " + ft.method1());      //3
      System.out.println("method2 returns " + ft.method2());      //4
    }
}
```

Executing this code reveals one obvious result, and one not so obvious. This code simply calls two methods, method1 and method2, and prints the values they return. The call at //3 to method1 results in 2 being printed. The catch block in method2 is never executed because an exception is not thrown. However, the call to method2 at //4 produces 4. The output from this code is:

```
method1 returns 2
method2 returns 4
```

This output is generated because finally blocks are always executed regardless of what happens in a try block. In this case, the value 3 is about to be returned at //1. On the execution of the return statement, however, control is transferred to the finally block at //2. This causes the return 4; statement to execute, which results in method2 returning the integer 4.

Traditionally, programmers think that when they execute a return statement they immediately leave the method they are executing. In Java, this is no longer true with the usage of finally. (A finally block is also entered on a break or continue statement that is executing inside of a try block.) This particular characteristic of finally has the potential to cause confusion and lead to long debugging sessions.

To avoid this pitfall, be sure you do not issue a return, break, or continue statement inside of a try block. If you cannot avoid this, be sure the existence of a finally does not change the return value of your method. This particular problem can arise during maintenance of your code, even with careful design and implementation. Good comments and careful code reviews ward it off.

PRAXIS 23: Place try/catch blocks outside of loops

Exceptions can have a negative impact on the performance of your code. Whether exceptions negatively affect performance has to do with how you structure your code and whether your JVM uses a JIT compiler that optimizes your code as it runs. Here are two areas of exceptions and performance to consider:

- The effect of throwing an exception

- The effects of try/catch blocks in your code

The act of throwing an exception is not free. After all, what are Java exceptions? They are objects and objects need to be created. Creating objects is costly (see PRAXIS 32), so, throwing an exception has costs. To throw an exception, you write something similar to this:

```
throw new MyException;
```

This code creates a new object and then transfers control to a catch or finally block or to the calling method. Because throwing exceptions entails some cost, use exceptions only for error conditions. When exceptions are used for control flow, the code is not as efficient or clear as it will be if typical flow constructs are used (see PRAXIS 24). Limit using exceptions for error and failure conditions. You want code to run fast when it works and typically do not care how long it takes to fail.

When considering the performance aspects of Java, you must take into account the JVM and operating system being utilized. Differences in execution times are observed between JVM's that are running identical code. Therefore, you must perform some level of profiling on your systems to determine the performance differences. The performance data in this PRAXIS was generated with the hardware and software setup detailed on page 98.

Placing try/catch blocks inside of loops can slow down the execution of code as the following code illustrates:

```
class ExcPerf
{
  public void method1(int size)
  {
    int[] ia = new int[size];
    try {
      for (int i=0; i<size; i++)
        ia[i] = i;
```

```
      }
      catch (Exception e) {} //Exception ignored on purpose
    }

    public void method2(int size)
    {
      int[] ia = new int[size];
      for (int i=0; i<size; i++)
      {
        try {
            ia[i] = i;
        }
        catch (Exception e) {}  //Exception ignored on purpose
      }
    }
  }
```

The methods, method1 and method2, contain almost identical code. The code in method1 has a try/catch block outside of its for loop, whereas the code in method2 has a try/catch block inside of its for loop. Note that neither method ever throws an exception. They simply have a try/catch block surrounding some code.

Running this code with the JIT compiler turned on results in no difference between the execution times of the methods. However, if you run this code with the JIT compiler turned off or with a JVM without a JIT, method2 is approximately 21 percent slower than method1.

This might lead you to believe that the generated bytecode for the two methods differ vastly. In fact, it is identical, except that the bytecode for method2 contains a few extra opcodes for the try/catch block inside of the loop. When run with a JIT compiler, this code is optimized to have no effect on its runtime. Without a JIT, however, each iteration of the loop incurs the cost of an extra branch. The following is the generated bytecode for both methods:

```
Method void method1(int)
    0 iload_1             //Push the value stored at index 1 of the
                          //local variable table(size) on the stack.
    1 newarray int        //Pop the size parameter and create a new
                          //int array with size elements. Push the
                          //newly created array reference(ia).
    3 astore_2            //Pop the array reference(ia) and store it
                          //at index 2 of the local variable table.
    4 iconst_0            //Beginning of try block. Push 0 for the
                          //initial value of the loop counter(i).
    5 istore_3            //Pop 0(i) and store it at index 3 of the
```

```
    ┌─ 6 goto 16            //local variable table.
    │                       //Jump to location 16.
    │   9 aload_2 ◄────┐    //Push the object reference(ia) at index 2
    │                  │    //of the local variable table.
    │  10 iload_3      │    //Push the value at index 3(i).
    │  11 iload_3      │    //Push the value at index 3(i).
    │  12 iastore      │    //Pop the top three values. Store the value
    │                  │    //of i at index i in the array(ia).
    │  13 iinc 3 1     │    //Increment the loop counter(i) stored at
    │                  │    //index 3 of the local variable table by 1.
    └─►16 iload_3      │    //Push the value at index 3(i).
       17 iload_1      │    //Push the value at index 1(size).
       18 if_icmplt 9 ─┘    //Pop both the loop counter(i) and size.
                            //Jump to location 9 if i is less than size.
       21 goto 25           //End of try block. Jump to location 25.
       24 pop               //Beginning of catch block.
       25 return            //Return from method.
    Exception table:        //If a java.lang.Exception occurs between
    from  to  target type   //location 4(inclusive) and location
      4   21    24   <Class java.lang.Exception>
                            //21(exclusive) jump to location 24.
```

```
    Method void method2(int)
       0 iload_1            //Push the value stored at index 1 of the
                            //local variable table(size) on the stack.
       1 newarray int       //Pop the size parameter and create a new
                            //int array with size elements. Push the
                            //newly created array reference(ia).
       3 astore_2           //Pop the array reference(ia) and store it
                            //at index 2 of the local variable table.
       4 iconst_0           //Push 0 for the initial value of the loop
                            //counter(i).
       5 istore_3           //Pop 0(i) and store it at index 3 of the
                            //local variable table.
    ┌─ 6 goto 23            //Jump to location 23.
    │   9 aload_2 ◄────┐    //Beginning of try block. Push the object
    │                  │    //reference(ia) at index 2.
    │  10 iload_3      │    //Push the value at index 3(i).
    │  11 iload_3      │    //Push the value at index 3(i).
    │  12 iastore      │    //Pop the top three values. Store the value
    │                  │    //of i at index i in the array(ia).
    │  13 goto 20      │    //End of try block. Jump to location 20.
    │  16 pop          │    //Beginning of catch block.
    │  17 goto 20      │    //Jump to location 20.
    │  20 iinc 3 1     │    //Increment the loop counter(i) stored at
    │                  │    //index 3 of the local variable table by 1.
    └─►23 iload_3      │    //Push the value at index 3(i).
       24 iload_1      │    //Push the value at index 1(size).
       25 if_icmplt 9 ─┘    //Pop both the loop counter(i) and size.
                            //Jump to location 9 if i is less than size.
       28 return           //Return from method.
```

```
Exception table:      //If a java.lang.Exception occurs between
from  to  target type //location 9(inclusive) and location
  9   13    16    <Class java.lang.Exception>
                      //13(exclusive) jump to location 16.
```

The arrows show the loop constructs for the two methods. Because of these differences, a better programming practice is to place `try/catch` blocks outside of loops. Your clients might be using a JVM without a JIT or, because of memory considerations, might be running with the JIT turned off. Therefore, you cannot assume that `try/catch` blocks inside of loops do not negatively affect code performance.

To run a file named `Test.class` with the JIT turned off, execute the following:

```
java -Djava.compiler=NONE Test
```

This disables the JIT on the JVM in use while the program `Test` runs.

PRAXIS 24: Do not use exceptions for control flow

Using exceptions for control flow is a bad idea. The flow through your code is expressed more clearly with the standard language constructs provided by Java. Consider the following code:

```java
class DoneWithLoopException extends Exception
{}

class Test
{
  public void foo()
  {
    //...
    try {
      while(true)
      {
        //Do something...
        if (some loop terminating condition)
          throw new DoneWithLoopException();
      }
    }
    catch (DoneWithLoopException e)
    {}
    //...
  }
}
```

This code uses exception handling for control flow. Instead of using normal loop break conditions, it uses exceptions to terminate the loop. The code works, but it is inefficient, unclear, and difficult to maintain. When you see code written like this, rewrite it properly. Use exception handling for exceptional conditions, not for flow control through your program.

PRAXIS 25: Do not use exceptions for every error condition

Exception handling was devised as a robust replacement for traditional error handling techniques. Given this, some programmers believe that exception handling should be used for any and all error conditions and that traditional error handling procedures should be avoided.

One can overuse exception handling. It should not be used for control flow (see PRAXIS 24) or to report conditions that are not errors. Exception handling should be used in conjunction with traditional error handling techniques to create efficient and easy to understand code.

The following is a comparison of the two styles, first using traditional error handling techniques and then using exceptions for all error conditions. The following code uses traditional return code error checking:

```
int data;
MyInputStream in = new MyInputStream("filename.ext");
data = in.getData();
while (data != 0)                                          //1
{
  //Do something with data
  data = in.getData();
}
```

Notice at //1 that the code checks to see whether the data value returned from the getData method call is nonzero. If it is zero, then you can assume that you are at the end of the stream and can therefore terminate the loop. This makes sense and is intuitive. Now, change this code to take a strict stance on exception handling. In this case, you do not rely on return code values, as is done previously, but instead use exceptions. The following code contains the original code with exception handling added:

```
int data;
MyInputStream in = new MyInputStream("filename.ext");
```

```
while(true)
{
  try {                                          //1
    data = in.getData();
  }
  catch (NoMoreDataException e1) {break;}
  //Do something with data
}
```

Notice at //1 that a try/catch block is placed around the call to the getData method. The getData method no longer returns zero when the stream is empty, but rather throws a NoMoreDataException. Although this code is a bit uglier than the original code, some programmers believe that code should be written in this manner. They argue that code that can utilize exceptions should no longer use traditional error handling techniques.

The code without the exceptions is much more intuitive, although it relies on the older methods to deal with errors or unexpected results. Exceptions can be overused, as the latter code example illustrates.

Use exceptions for conditions outside of the expected behavior of the code. In the previous examples, you expect to get to the end of the stream, so a simple zero return from the getData method is appropriate and natural. Throwing an exception in this case is unwise, since this is not an exceptional condition but rather an expected one. You do not, however, expect the stream to be corrupted. That type of condition calls for an exception to be generated. The point is not to use exceptions for all conditions, but to use them where it makes sense, that is, where exceptional conditions exist.

The exclusive use of exceptions, as in the second example, might make your program "pure" as far as exceptions are concerned. However, you have used exceptions for every error condition. Simply returning zero is much faster and more intuitive than creating an exception object and requiring the caller to implement a catch block to handle it.

PRAXIS 26: Throw exceptions from constructors

Traditional error reporting from constructors can be problematic because a constructor has no return value. Thus, you cannot simply return an error code when a constructor fails. True, constructors are not methods, but you are not precluded from throwing an exception from a constructor.

Error reporting from constructors has typically been accomplished via several techniques. One technique is *two-stage construction*, whereby code that potentially generates errors is moved out of the constructor and into methods where return codes can be used. The drawback to this technique is that the user of the class must call the constructor, then call the method that can potentially generate the errors, and then check the return code or catch an exception.

An alternative to two-stage construction is to use an internal flag on the constructed object. This flag represents the object's validity after it has been constructed. For example, if the constructor finishes without errors, it sets a flag in the object to indicate that the object is valid and therefore can be used reliably. If the constructor fails for some reason, the flag is set to indicate that the object is invalid and thus cannot be used reliably.

This internal flag is then used in either one of two ways. In the first way, users of the object need to call a method of the class that checks the flag for validity before invoking any other methods on the object. In the second way, each method of the object first calls this method to determine validity. If the object is invalid, an error is returned or an exception is thrown. This guarantees that methods do not execute on invalid objects.

All of these techniques lack robustness. They require the user of the class to remember to perform the two-stage construction or call a special method to test for the validity of the object, or require each method call to incur the overhead of checking an internal state flag.

You avoid all of this by throwing exceptions from your constructors. Consider the following code:

```java
import java.io.*;

class Foo
{
  public Foo (String fileName) throws FileNotFoundException,
                                     IOException
  {
    FileReader fr = new FileReader(fileName);
    BufferedReader br = new BufferedReader(fr);
    String str = br.readLine();
    //...
  }
  public void scanfile()
  {}
}
```

```
class Test
{
  public static void main(String args[])
  {
    Foo somefoo = null;
    try {
      somefoo = new Foo("temp.fil");
    }
    catch (FileNotFoundException fnfe) { //Catch constructor
      //...                                  //failure
    }
    catch (IOException ioe) {  //Catch constructor failure
      //...
    }
    //Use somefoo
    somefoo.scanfile();
  }
}
```

The constructor for class Foo receives a String argument which represents a filename. It then attempts to open the file that has that filename. If the filename is invalid, the constructor generates a FileNotFoundException. If the file is available, the code attempts to read from it. However, reading from the file could generate an IOException. Because the constructor does not handle these exceptions, it must list them on its throws clause (see PRAXES 19 and 20).

The code creating the Foo class wraps the call to the Foo constructor with a try/catch block to handle any potential failures. As an added benefit to this approach, if the constructor throws an exception and the handling code ignores the exception, the local variable somefoo is set to null. This is because it is not properly constructed and therefore cannot be used reliably. Attempts to access the somefoo variable result in the Java runtime generating a NullPointerException.

Although constructors are not methods, they can still generate exceptions and support the throws clause. This technique for dealing with constructor failures is your most robust and effective option, requiring the least amount of manual intervention on behalf of the programmer using your class.

PRAXIS 27: Return objects to a valid state before throwing an exception

Throwing an exception is easy. The hard part is to minimize the damage you cause by throwing one. Too often programmers are led to believe that error handling begins and ends with the keywords try, throw, catch, throws, and finally. Proper error handling only begins with these.

Ask yourself, what is the purpose of throwing an exception? The explicit purpose is to inform another part of your system about a problem. The implicit purpose is for the software that catches the exception to potentially recover from the problem and keep the system running. If the system recovers and continues running after an exception is generated, the code that generated the exception could be reentered. Objects whose states were altered prior to an exception being thrown will be used again as the system continues to run. The looming questions are what are the states of these objects and will the system run correctly after an exception is thrown?

What good is it to throw an exception if you leave objects in invalid or undefined states? If your objects are left in a bad state, then the code, upon recovery of the exception, very likely will fail anyway. Before throwing exceptions, you must think about in what states your objects are currently. If they are in states such that the code fails even if the exception is recovered from, consider what has to be done to place them in valid states before throwing the exception.

Typically, programmers assume that code in a method will finish without errors. When an error occurs, many or all of the assumptions that have been made are not valid. For example, consider the following code:

```
class SomeException extends Exception
{}
class MyList
{}
class Foo
{
  private int numElements;
  private MyList myList;

  public void add(Object o) throws SomeException
  {
    //...
    numElements++;                                    //1
    if (myList.maxElements() < numElements)
    {
      //Reallocate myList
      //Copy elements as necessary
      //Could throw exceptions
    }
    myList.addToList(o);  //Could throw exception      //2
  }
}
```

This code contains an add method that adds an object to a list. The method first increases a counter at //1 for the number of objects in the list. It then conditionally reallocates the list and adds the object to the list at //2. This code is seriously flawed. Notice that the code between //1 and the addToList call at //2 can throw exceptions. If an exception is thrown after //1, then the object is now in an invalid state because the counter, numElements, is incorrect. If the caller of this method recovers from the thrown exception and calls this method again, other problems likely will arise because the object state is invalid.

Fixing this particular problem is simple:

```
class Foo
{
  private int numElements;
  private MyList myList;

  public void add(Object o) throws SomeException
  {
    //...
    if (myList.maxElements() == numElements)               //1
    {
      //Reallocate myList
      //Copy elements as necessary
      //Could throw exceptions
    }
    myList.addToList(o);  //Could throw exception
    numElements++;                                         //2
  }
}
```

To fix the problem, simply change your test at //1 and move the increment of numElements to the end of the method at //2. This ensures that the counter, numElements, is accurate because you increment it after you have successfully added the object to the list. This is a simple example, but it exposes a potentially serious problem.

You must worry about not only the object you are currently running in, but also other objects you might have modified in your method. For example, you might have completely or partially created a file, opened a socket, or made remote method calls to another machine when an exception occurs. You need to be aware of the state of all affected objects, and of the system itself, if you expect your code to work properly when reentered. For example, consider the following:

```
import java.io.IOException;

class MutualFund
{
  public void buyMoreShares(double money)
  {}
  //...
}

class Customer
{
  private MutualFund[] fundArray;

  public Customer()
  {}

  public MutualFund[] funds()
  {
    return fundArray;
  }

  public void updateMutualFund(MutualFund fund) throws
    DatabaseException
  {}

  public void writePortfolioChange() throws IOException
  {}
  //...
}

class DatabaseException extends Exception
{}

class Services
{
  public void invest(Customer cust, double money) throws
    IOException, DatabaseException
  {
    MutualFund[] array = cust.funds();                        //1
    int size = array.length;

    for (int i=0; i<size; i++)
    {
      ((MutualFund)array[i]).buyMoreShares(money);            //2
      cust.updateMutualFund(array[i]);
      cust.writePortfolioChange();
    }
    //...
  }
}
```

The invest method invests money for a customer in each of the customer's mutual fund accounts. The Customer class contains a funds method that returns an array of all funds held by the customer. The invest method invests the same amount of money to each fund held by the customer via the buyMoreShares method. The code then updates the MutualFund object in a database and makes a portfolio change to the Customer object. This portfolio change creates a record of the account activity so the customer is notified about the transaction. The last two methods in the loop can potentially fail and throw an exception. Because the invest method does not handle the exceptions, they are listed in the throws clause in order to avoid a compiler error.

Some programmers write this type of code, test it, determine that it works properly, and think they are finished. When testing the code, they find that if one of the methods fails, the appropriate exception is thrown and the method exits as expected. Depending on the thoroughness of their testing, they might not find the other problems that lurk here.

Whenever you have code that generates exceptions, you need to ask yourself what happens if an exception occurs, is handled, and the code is then reentered. Will the code work properly? In this case, this code has problems.

Assume a particular customer owns shares in three mutual funds and wants to buy $1,000 more of each. The fund array is accessed at //1 and $1,000 of shares are purchased of the first fund in the array at //2. The updated fund is then successfully written to a database using the updateMutualFund method. You then call the writePortfolioChange method, which writes some information to a file. This method fails, however, because there is not enough disk space to create the file. Thus, an exception is thrown and the method exits abruptly before completing all three steps on the first MutualFund object.

Assume the caller of the invest method properly handles the exception by freeing some disk space and then calls the invest method again. When the invest method executes a second time, the fund array is accessed at //1 and then the loop is entered to buy more shares of each fund. Remember that you have already purchased $1,000 of more shares of the first fund when you called the invest method initially. However, you are about to do it again. Assuming the invest method completes successfully for this customer's three funds, you have incorrectly purchased $2,000 of shares of the first fund and $1,000 of shares of the other two funds. Obviously, this is not what is desired.

You handled the exception properly with regard to freeing some disk space and then called the method again. What you did not do was pay attention to the object state when you exited the invest method after the exception was thrown.

One solution to fix this problem requires that you add methods in the MutualFund and Customer classes that are called when exceptions are processed in the invest method. These methods reverse what occurred in the event that the code did not complete successfully. Furthermore, catch blocks are added to the invest method to handle any exceptions generated. These catch blocks call the appropriate methods to reset the object state so the method can succeed properly if called again. The modified code looks like this:

```java
import java.io.IOException;

class MutualFund
{
  public void buyMoreShares(double money)
  {}
  public void sellShares(double money)
  {}
  //...
}

class Customer
{
  private MutualFund[] fundArray;

  public Customer()
  {}

  public MutualFund[] funds()
  {
    return fundArray;
  }

  public void updateMutualFund(MutualFund fund) throws
    DatabaseException
  {}
  public void undoMutualFundUpdate(MutualFund fund)
  {}

  public void writePortfolioChange() throws IOException
  {}
  //...
}

class DatabaseException extends Exception
{}
```

```
class Services
{
  public void invest(Customer cust, double money) throws
    IOException, DatabaseException
  {
    MutualFund[] array = cust.funds();
    int size = array.length;

    for (int i=0; i<size; i++)
    {
      ((MutualFund)array[i]).buyMoreShares(money);
      try {
        cust.updateMutualFund(array[i]);
      }
      catch(DatabaseException dbe)  //Catch exception and return
      {                            //object to a valid state.
        ((MutualFund)array[i]).sellShares(money);
        throw dbe;
      }
      try {
        cust.writePortfolioChange();
      }
      catch(IOException ioe)  //Catch exception and return object
      {                       //to a valid state.
        ((MutualFund)array[i]).sellShares(money);
        cust.undoMutualFundUpdate(array[i]);
        throw ioe;
      }
    }
    //...
  }
}
```

This code now works as expected if an exception is thrown and the method is reentered. So that this code would work properly, a method was added to the MutualFund and Customer classes, thereby enabling operations on these objects to be undone in the event of an exception. The loop in the invest method was also changed to catch the exceptions that could occur and to then reset the object state. After the object state is valid and the code works if reentered, the exceptions are rethrown so the calling methods can attempt recovery.

This code is much more difficult to write and follow than is its original form, but these types of steps are necessary to create code that is robust and can recover from exceptions.

Another issue to consider is what happens if your recovery methods, sellShares and undoMutualFundUpdate, fail. To keep the system running, you need to deal with these failures. As you can see, leaving objects in a valid state when throwing exceptions can be extremely difficult.

If you expect callers of your code to recover from the exceptions you generate, you want to look at all of the places where exceptions can occur. If the method exits abruptly where the exceptions occur, then you need to examine whether you leave your objects in states so that if the method is entered again the correct results are generated. If you are not leaving objects in a valid state, you need to take measures to ensure that reentering your code works properly and as expected.

The process described in this PRAXIS resembles a transaction. With a transaction, you need a commit and rollback plan. If all of the parts of the transaction do not complete properly, then the entire transaction is canceled. You might want to consider a global transaction or commit and rollback strategy to implement a solution to this problem.

Unfortunately, solving these types of problems is extremely difficult and time consuming. To implement these solutions properly takes not only programming time and extensive testing, but also a lot of hard thinking. It takes much more work and effort to address these problems after the code is written than it does to keep these issues in mind during design and initial coding.

Performance

Many things difficult to design prove easy to performance.
—Samuel Johnson, *Rasselas*, Chapter xvi.

PERFORMANCE receives more focus and attention than any other aspect of Java. Many believe that it must be "fixed" in order to ensure Java's continued success. However, "fixing" Java performance is not the sole responsibility of compiler and JVM providers. Programmers who write Java code must also provide some of the solutions. This is because some performance problems that are labeled as Java performance problems are actually design problems. They have nothing to do with Java.

It is not only that Java can be slow. Poorly designed or poorly written code also can be slow. Java is getting faster due to the progress being made with JIT code generators, garbage collection, and other runtime optimizations. These advances in runtime performance technology, however, do not absolve programmers from using sound programming techniques. Poorly designed code still runs slowly no matter how many loops are unrolled or how many variables are placed in hardware registers. A bubble sort is still an $O(n^2)$ algorithm regardless of how much tuning and tweaking is done. The first step to fast code is properly designed code.

Notwithstanding the advances and improvements in runtime optimization technology, you can use proven techniques that have a positive impact on Java runtime performance. No miracle performance cures are presented here, simply because they do not exist. This section instead examines several design and coding techniques that make Java code smaller and execute faster. With any optimization technique, remember that the technique, used alone, might not have a great impact on performance. Several techniques used in conjunction, however, can produce significant performance gains. The information presented in this section, applied properly, will make your code faster.

Before reading this section, keep a few things in mind about optimization:

- Do not optimize code unless you have proved that optimization is necessary. The only way to prove this is with your own timing technique or an execution profiler.

- Unless optimization is done very carefully, you can introduce bugs into your code. Slow code that works is better than fast code that breaks.

- After performing an optimization, profile again to prove that it has the desired effect.

- There is no common cost model for JVMs. Therefore, a technique that results in faster code on one JVM will not necessarily give the same results on another JVM.

All information presented in this section, whether performance numbers or generated bytecode listings, was generated with the following hardware and software configuration:

- IBM Thinkpad 600E

- Pentium II processor running at 300 Mhz

- 160 MB of memory

- Windows NT 4.0 with Service Pack 4

- Sun Java 2 SDK, Standard Edition, v1.2.1.

Wherever a reference to performance characteristics of code is made, these characteristics are determined through the following timing technique:

```
long start = System.currentTimeMillis();
//Code to time
long end = System.currentTimeMillis();
long time = end - start;
```

In addition, all performance improvement techniques presented in this section result in faster code when the previously given hardware and software configuration is used. Before applying a technique, verify that it actually results in faster code on your configuration.

PRAXIS 28: **Focus initially on design, data structures, and algorithms**

> *We should forget about small efficiencies, about 97% of the time. Premature optimization is the root of all evil.*
> —Donald E. Knuth, *Literate Programming*, p. 28

Too often, programmers, in a quest for fast code, forgo a solid design for perceived and yet unrealized, performance improvements. In an effort to generate the fastest and smallest possible code from the beginning, they make bad design trade-offs. While this approach might produce fast code, it more likely will result in code that is less efficient and a design that lacks robustness, extensibility, and maintainability. Furthermore, application of such an approach requires programmers to guess, at design time, where performance problems might be without the benefit of having running code and empirical data.

When it comes time to modify your code to make it run faster, the changes required are much easier and less costly if you begin with a solid design. Modifying code of a poorly designed program is extremely time consuming and error prone. Therefore, focus your energies on the creation of a good, solid design that can be modified later, if necessary, to achieve your performance objectives.

The PRAXES in this section contain various techniques to get Java to perform faster. Some of this information you should use and incorporate at design time. Other information should be used after you have code running, and only if you do not meet your performance objectives.

Some of the advice is general and can be applied to any implementation without compromising a design. Some is very specific and should be used only in certain areas of code that need attention. For example, no design should include the use of the String class for concatenations when the StringBuffer class will suffice (see PRAXIS 31). Also, every loop that is written should not automatically be unrolled (see PRAXIS 44). The time to unroll a loop is when you know that doing so provides a significant enough performance boost to warrant the risk, effort, and extra code it requires.

You should also consider whether you are creating an application or a class library. If you are creating an application, you have the luxury of using a performance profiler on your code and generating profiling data. This enables you to optimize your code after you are finished implementing the application. It also allows you to reliably determine what parts of the application need attention.

If you are creating a class library, you normally do not know all of the ways in which an application programmer might use it. This makes it difficult to determine what optimizations should be done and where they should be applied. You can use a profiler, but the data it generates depends on your guess at how the application programmer will use your library. Therefore, it is difficult to generate performance data that is representative of how someone will use your classes. In this case, you might want to incorporate more optimizations up front than you otherwise would for an application.

One rule for producing fast code is to optimize only what you must. Time spent optimizing code that does not have a substantive impact on the performance of your program is time wasted. Typically, 80 to 90 percent of the execution time of a program is spent executing 10 to 20 percent of its code. The 10 to 20 percent of your code that needs improvement is best found by using performance profilers.

Remember, efficient code has more to do with good design and sage choices of data structures and algorithms than with the implementation language. This section does not attempt to replicate these generic techniques. There already are many good books on these subjects. For example, start with *Design Patterns: Elements of Reusable Object-Oriented Software*[1] or the *Design Patterns CD.*[2] Another book is *The Practice of Programming.*[3] Chapters 2 and 7 are particularly relevant to this discussion.

In summary, the biggest performance improvements are made to Java not by using specific Java performance tips, many of which are presented in the following PRAXES, but by using time-honored, language-independent techniques in design and algorithms. Some of the performance information presented here should be used only *after* you have a good design with appropriate data structures and algorithms and have generated reliable data with a performance profiler. Many of the individual PRAXES can then be used to fine-tune your code when sufficient empirical data proves the need for further modification.

---

[1] *Design Patterns: Elements of Reusable Object-Oriented Software*, Erich Gamma, Richard Helm, Ralph Johnson, John Vlissides, Addison-Wesley, 1995.

[2] *Design Patterns CD: Elements of Reusable Object-Oriented Software*, Erich Gamma, Richard Helm, Ralph Johnson, John Vlissides, Addison-Wesley, 1998.

[3] *The Practice of Programming*, Brian W. Kernighan and Rob Pike, Addison-Wesley, 1999.

PRAXIS 29: **Do not rely on compile-time code optimization**

Most programmers are accustomed to compilers from other languages that support optimizations. Typically in development, your code is compiled with optimizations turned off so that a source-level debugger works properly. When you have the code debugged, you turn on compiler optimizations to get the fastest possible code produced from the compiler. The optimized code is generally very different from the unoptimized code. This is because modern compiler optimization technology is fairly advanced and rearranges code so that it executes faster.

This causes some programmers to inadvertently rely on the optimization features of compilers to clean up sloppily written code. This is never a good idea, although a good compiler can hide certain coding inefficiencies. For example, consider the following carelessly coded C++ loop:

```
int a = 10;
int b = 20;
int *arr = new int[10];
for (i=0; i<10; i++)
  arr[i] = a + b;
```

Because a and b are invariant and do not change inside of the loop, their addition need not be performed for each loop iteration. Almost any good compiler optimizes this code. An optimizer moves the addition of a and b outside of the loop, thereby making the loop more efficient. For example, the optimized code has the same structure as the following C++ code:

```
int a = 10;
int b = 20;
int *arr = new int[10];
int c = a + b;
for (i=0; i<10; i++)
  arr[i] = c;
```

This is a common, yet simple example. Optimizations can be very complex. You might be surprised, however, that many Java compilers do little in the way of optimization. The Sun Java compiler, javac, and most other Java compilers, support only a few minor optimizations. Included in the supported optimizations are simple constant folding and simple dead code elimination.

Constant folding involves the compiler precalculating constant expressions. Consider this code:

```
static final int length = 10;
static final int width = 5;
int value = length * width;
```

Instead of execution time being spent multiplying these values, multiplication is done at compile time. This code is converted to bytecode of the form:

```
int value = 50;
```

Simple dead code elimination involves having the compiler not generate bytecode for blocks that are never executed. Dead code elimination does not affect the code's runtime execution. It does, however, reduce the size of the generated .class file. For example, the two expressions in method foo are not converted to bytecode:

```
class Test
{
  public static final boolean trace = false;
  public void foo()
  {
    if (Test.trace)
      //...

    if (false)
      //...
  }
}
```

Of course, code is still generated if an expression *evaluates* to false at runtime. The only case in which the bytecode is not generated is when the expression evaluates to false at compile time.

The Java 2 SDK documentation for javac states that the –O option will "Optimize code for execution time." If you think this option gives you all of the optimization benefits of languages such as FORTRAN, C, and C++, think again. To illustrate, look at how the previous code with the loop invariant, written in Java, is compiled with javac –O. The Java source code looks like this:

```
class Test
{
  public static void main(String args[])
  {
    int a = 10;
    int b = 20;
    int[] arr = new int[10];
```

```
    for (int i=0; i<10; i++)
      arr[i] = a + b;
  }
}
```

Compiling this code with javac -O produces a .class file. This .class file is disassembled with javap -c and produces the following, supposedly optimized, generated bytecode for method main:

```
Method void main(java.lang.String[])
    0 bipush 10         //Push 10 on the stack.
    2 istore_1          //Pop 10 and store it at index 1 of the
                        //local variable table(a).
    3 bipush 20         //Push 20 on the stack.
    5 istore_2          //Pop 20 and store it at index 2 of the
                        //local variable table(b).
    6 bipush 10         //Push 10 for the size of the int array.
    8 newarray int      //Pop 10 and create a new int array with 10
                        //elements. Push the newly created array
                        //reference(arr).
   10 astore_3          //Pop the array reference(arr) and store it
                        //at index 3 of the local variable table.
   11 iconst_0          //Push 0 for the initial value of the loop
                        //counter(i).
   12 istore 4          //Pop 0(i) and store it at index 4 of the
                        //local variable table.
   14 goto 27           //Jump to location 27.
   17 aload_3           //Push the object reference(arr) at index 3
                        //of the local variable table.
   18 iload 4           //Push the value at index 4(i).
   20 iload_1           //Push the value at index 1(a==10).
   21 iload_2           //Push the value at index 2(b==20).
   22 iadd              //Pop the top two values (10 and 20), add
                        //them, and push the result(30).
   23 iastore           //Pop the top three values. Store 30 at
                        //index i in the array(arr).
   24 iinc 4 1          //Increment the loop counter(i) stored at
                        //index 4 of the local variable table by 1.
   27 iload 4           //Push the value at index 4(i).
   29 bipush 10         //Push 10 (the loop terminator value).
   31 if_icmplt 17      //Pop both i and 10. Jump to location 17 if
                        //i is less than 10.
   34 return            //Return from method.
```

Notice the bytecode that adds a and b is still inside the for loop. (The arrows highlight the for loop construct.) Turning on optimization did not move this invariant code outside of the loop as expected. In fact, for this code the .class file and generated bytecode are identical when compiled without optimization. In other words, turning on optimization had no effect on the generated code.

So, just what does the –0 option for javac do? Its functions vary depending on the particular compiler used. However, used with the Sun Java 2 SDK compiler it has absolutely no effect on the generated code. Thus, using the –0 option is meaningless despite what the documentation says.

Several sources indicate that the Java compiler provides method inlining.[4] Methods are considered candidates for inlining when they are small and can be statically resolved by the compiler. Methods that can be statically resolved are methods that cannot be overridden. Methods that cannot be overridden are private, static, and final. Consider the following code compiled with javac:

```java
class Foo
{
  final public int bar1()
  {
    return 1;
  }
  public int bar2()
  {
    return bar4();              //Call to private bar4 not inlined.
  }
  static public int bar3()
  {
    return 3;
  }
  private int bar4()
  {
    return 4;
  }
}

class Test
{
  public static void main(String args[])
  {
    Foo f = new Foo();
    int a = 5 + f.bar1();       //Call to final bar1 not inlined.
    int b = 5 + f.bar2();
    int c = 5 + Foo.bar3();     //Call to static bar3 not inlined.
  }
}
```

----

4. Previous releases of the Sun Java compiler performed some method inlining. This optimization has since been removed.

A cursory examination of the bytecode for this code shows that none of the methods that are candidates for inlining is inlined, and each is left as a distinct method call. These methods are, however, inlined by the JIT at runtime.

Because the –0 compiler option of the Sun Java 2 SDK compiler has no effect on the generated code, there is currently no need to use it. Therefore, the generated code is no better than what you write. (See PRAXIS 44 for various ways to hand-optimize your Java source to generate better and faster executing bytecode.) In addition, do not assume other vendor's Java compilers perform optimizations beyond the most trivial cases.

Programmers need to understand that few optimizations are performed by typical Java compilers. For those that compilers do not perform, programmers have three options:

1. Hand-optimize the Java source code in an attempt to achieve better performance (see PRAXIS 44).

2. Use a third-party optimizing compiler that compiles Java source to optimized bytecode (see PRAXIS 45).

3. Rely on runtime optimizations such as JITs or Hotspot.

As third-party compilers improve and gain acceptance, other major compiler vendors might improve the compilers in the tools you currently use. Until then, you are left with these options.

PRAXIS 30: **Understand runtime code optimization**

PRAXIS 29 discusses the fact that most Java compilers do not generate optimized bytecode. Certain JITs, however, do perform various optimizations. The purpose of a JIT is to convert bytecode to native binary code at runtime. In addition, some JITs analyze and perform some optimization on the bytecode prior to converting it to binary code. Most, if not all, JVMs for desktop and enterprise systems come with a JIT that runs by default. For instance, in the examples in PRAXIS 29, the methods would be inlined and the loop invariant moved outside of the loop.

JITs improve performance by replacing interpretive execution of bytecode with native execution of binary code. Native execution is typically much faster than interpretive execution. Therefore, if the compiled code is executed a sufficient number of times, the cost of generating the native code is justified. However, it is very difficult for a JIT to determine how much optimization it should perform. It must make sure that the time needed to collect the data and perform the optimization does not exceed the time the optimization is going to save.

Most of the time, running your code with a good JIT results in faster executing code. What some programmers tend to forget is that the JIT must run—this consumes execution time. In addition, JITs are designed to run for a relatively short amount of time because they exist to speed up your code and not to slow it down. Therefore, JITs must skip many valuable optimizations due to the time it takes to collect sufficient data needed to perform them.

Some programmers believe there is no need for a Java compiler to spend time optimizing bytecode because certain JITs optimize where the Java compiler has not. However, consider that the more work a JIT must do, the longer it runs. The longer it runs, the longer your program runs. If the Java compiler does not optimize even simple cases, more work is left for the JIT to do. This can negatively affect your code's performance. Unlike a JIT, the Java compiler can afford to spend extra time performing advanced optimizations without detracting from the code's runtime performance.

Much of the effort involved in Java performance enhancements centers around runtime optimizations. This is unfortunate because opportunities exist for Java compilers to optimize Java source code and generate optimized bytecode. Java compilers could perform some similar optimization techniques used in other languages.

Another problem with relying solely on runtime optimizations is size. As Java continues its growth in the embedded and real-time programming spaces, alternative optimization solutions must be used. Many embedded systems might not have enough memory available for a JIT or Hotspot runtime. For real-time programming, where Java is moving quickly, a JIT or Hotspot runtime creates problems because they increase non-deterministic behavior.[5]

A winning performance combination is optimized bytecode combined with a good JIT or Hotspot runtime. This enables the desktop, embedded, or real-time programmer to choose from the static or dynamic approach to optimization. This choice can be made depending on the needs and attributes of the specific system being written.

[5.] For more information on real-time Java, see www.rtj.org.

PRAXIS 31:   Use `StringBuffer`, rather than `String`, for concatenation

The Java library provides the `String` and `StringBuffer` classes. The `String` class is used to represent character strings that cannot be changed after they are created. In other words, objects of type `String` are read-only and immutable. The `StringBuffer` class is used to represent character strings that can be modified. It provides methods to modify the contents of the underlying character string, whereas the `String` class does not.

A key difference between these two classes is that `StringBuffer` is much faster than `String` when performing simple concatenation. It is easy to habitually use the `String` class and not to consider `StringBuffer`, even when a `StringBuffer` will suffice.

In most string manipulation code, character strings are routinely concatenated. Using the `String` class, concatenation is performed like this:

```
String str = new String("Practical ");
str += "Java";
```

Using `StringBuffer` for concatenation in this example results in code that looks like this:

```
StringBuffer str = new StringBuffer("Practical ");
str.append("Java");
```

Your first reaction might be that the first example using `String` is more efficient. You might surmise that because using a `StringBuffer` requires a call to the append method for each concatenation, this operation must be slower than simply using the + operator to concatenate two `String` objects. The + operator is innocent looking, however, the code it generates is not.

In fact, using a `StringBuffer` for concatenation in this code is several hundred times faster than using a `String`. To understand why, you need to examine the generated bytecode. The bytecode for the first example using a `String` looks like this:

```
0 new #7 <Class java.lang.String>
3 dup
4 ldc #2 <String "Practical ">
6 invokespecial #12 <Method java.lang.String(java.lang.String)>
```

```
 9 astore_1
10 new #8 <Class java.lang.StringBuffer>
13 dup
14 aload_1
15 invokestatic #23 <Method java.lang.String valueOf(
                                      java.lang.Object)>
18 invokespecial #13 <Method java.lang.StringBuffer(
                                      java.lang.String)>
21 ldc #1 <String "Java">
23 invokevirtual #15 <Method java.lang.StringBuffer append(
                                      java.lang.String)>
26 invokevirtual #22 <Method java.lang.String toString()>
29 astore_1
```

First, the bytecode at locations 0 through 9 is executed for the first line of code:

```
String str = new String("Practical ");
```

Then, the bytecode at locations 10 through 29 is executed for the concatenation:

```
str += "Java";
```

Notice that the generated bytecode for the concatenation creates a StringBuffer object and invokes its append method. A temporary StringBuffer object is created at location 10, and its append method is called at location 23. Because the String class is immutable, a StringBuffer must be used for the concatenation.

After the concatenation is performed on the StringBuffer object, it must be converted back to a String. This is done with the call to the toString method at location 26. This method creates a new String object from the temporary StringBuffer object. Note that the creation of the temporary StringBuffer object and its conversion back to a String object is very costly (see PRAXIS 32).

These two lines of code result in the creation of five objects: two String objects at locations 0, and 4, a StringBuffer object at location 10, and two more String objects at locations 21 and 26.

Compare this with the generated bytecode for the example using StringBuffer:

```
0 new #8 <Class java.lang.StringBuffer>
3 dup
4 ldc #2 <String "Practical ">
6 invokespecial #13 <Method java.lang.StringBuffer(
                                      java.lang.String)>
9 astore_1
```

```
10 aload_1
11 ldc #1 <String "Java">
13 invokevirtual #15 <Method java.lang.StringBuffer append(
                                                java.lang.String)>
16 pop
```

First, the bytecode at locations 0 through 9 is executed for the first line of code:

```
StringBuffer str = new StringBuffer("Practical ");
```

Then the bytecode at locations 10 through 16 is executed for the concatenation:

```
str.append("Java");
```

Notice that as with the first example, this code invokes the append method of a StringBuffer object. Unlike the first example, however, there is no need to create a temporary StringBuffer and then convert it to a String object. This code creates only three objects, a StringBuffer at location 0 and two String objects at locations 4 and 11.

As mentioned earlier, the StringBuffer concatenation is several hundred times faster than a String concatenation. Therefore, you should use StringBuffer for this operation whenever possible. If you need the functionality of the String class, consider using a StringBuffer for concatenations and then performing one conversion to String and accessing the needed methods of that class. Minimizing the number of conversions from a StringBuffer to a String reduces the number of objects created. This greatly improves code performance.

PRAXIS 32: **Minimize the cost of object creation**

Programmers writing code in an object-oriented language such as Java sometimes overlook the cost incurred to create objects. Creating an object is often much more expensive than programmers realize. Object construction is not simply allocating some memory and initializing a few fields. It can be a much more involved process. Therefore, it is wise to minimize the number and size of objects you create, especially in performance-critical code. Using a good, solid design is one way to minimize this (see PRAXIS 28). To understand the costs involved, look at what happens when an object is created.

Several things must happen in a particular order to ensure the object is constructed properly.

1. Memory is allocated from the heap to hold all instance variables and implementation-specific data of the object and its superclasses. Implementation-specific data includes pointers to class and method data.

2. The instance variables of the objects are initialized to their default values.

3. The constructor for the most derived class is invoked.[6] The first thing a constructor does is call the constructor for its superclass. This process continues until the constructor for `java.lang.Object` is invoked. (Remember that the `java.lang.Object` class is the base class for all objects in Java.)

4. Before the body of the constructor is executed, all instance variable initializers and initialization blocks are executed. Next, the body of the constructor is executed. Thus, the constructor for the base class completes first and the constructor for the most derived class completes last. This allows the constructor for a class to safely use the instance variables of any of its superclasses.

Given that all of this happens as a result of creating an object, creating a lightweight object is much faster than creating a heavyweight object. A lightweight object is an object that does not have a long inheritance chain and does not contain many other objects. A heavyweight object is an object that might have a long inheritance chain or might contain large objects. Heavyweight objects also might contain many lightweight objects. Consider the following lightweight class:

```
class Light
{
  private int val;
  private boolean hasData = true;
  public Light(int a)
  {
    val = a;
  }
  //...
}
```

[6.] In reality, the constructor is replaced by an initialization method in the `.class` file. The initialization method is a special method called `<init>` that is placed in the `.class` file by the Java compiler. It contains the code of the constructor, code to initialize the instance variables, and code to invoke the superclass initialization method.

This class does not explicitly extend any other class. Because all objects implicitly inherit from java.lang.Object, the superclass of Light is also its base class. Therefore, the length of its inheritance chain is very short. In addition, this class does not contain any data members that are objects. It does, however, contain two data members that are primitive types (see PRAXES 8 and 38). Following are the steps to create an object of the Light class with this invocation:

```
Light lgt = new Light(5);
```

1. Memory from the heap is allocated to store the instance variables of the Light class in addition to memory for any object implementation-specific data.[7]

2. The class's instance variable data members, val and hasData, are initialized to their default values. val is assigned the value 0 because that is the default value for an int, and hasData is initialized to its default value, false.

3. The constructor for the class Light is invoked with a value of 5.

4. The constructor for Light invokes its superclass constructor. The superclass is java.lang.Object.

5. When the constructor for java.lang.Object returns, the constructor for Light performs its instance variable initialization. In this case, hasData is assigned the value true.

6. The body of the Light constructor completes by assigning val the value 5.

7. The object reference, lgt, refers to the newly created Light object on the heap.

Contrast these steps with the creation of a heavyweight object. Consider the following class declarations:

```
import java.awt.*;
class Base
{
  private int val;
  public Base(int a)
  {
    val = a;
```

---

[7] The memory allocated also includes instance variables of the base class, java.lang. Object, if there are any. The representation of java.lang.Object is implementation-dependent. It is unlikely, however, that an implementation of java.lang.Object will contain any instance variables due to the overhead involved.

```
      }
  }
  class Der1 extends Base
  {
    public Der1(int a)
    {
      super(a);
    }
  }
  class Der2 extends Der1
  {
    private boolean state;
    private boolean hasData = true;
    public Der2(int a, boolean b)
    {
      super(a);
      state = b;
    }
  }
  class Heavy extends Der2
  {
    private Point pt;
    private TextField tf;
    public Heavy(int a, boolean b)
    {
      super(a, b);
      pt = new Point(0,0);
      tf = new TextField("text");
    }
    //...
  }
```

Creating an object of type Heavy is much more involved and time consuming. Following are the steps to create an object of the Heavy class, with this invocation:

```
Heavy hvy = new Heavy(4, true);
```

1. Memory from the heap is allocated to store the instance variables of classes Heavy (pt and tf), Der2 (state and hasData), and Base (val), as well as any object implementation-specific data.

2. The instance variable data members are initialized to their default values. Specifically, the object references, pt and tf, are assigned the value null. The boolean state and hasData variables are assigned the value false, and the primitive int val is assigned the value 0.

3. The constructor for class Heavy is invoked with the values 4 and true.

4. The constructor for Heavy immediately invokes the constructor for its super-class, Der2.

5. The constructor for Der2 immediately invokes the constructor for its super-class, Der1.

6. The constructor for Der1 immediately invokes the constructor for its super-class, Base.

7. The constructor for Base immediately invokes the constructor for its super-class, java.lang.Object.

8. When the constructor for java.lang.Object returns, the constructor for Base assigns the instance data, val, the value 4, and then returns.

9. The constructor for Der1 completes and returns.

10. The constructor for Der2 performs its instance variable initialization and assigns hasData the value true.

11. The constructor for Der2 executes and assigns state the value true and then returns.

12. The constructor for Heavy executes and attempts to create an object of the Point class and an object of the TextField class. Before these calls return, this entire process, beginning with Step 1, is repeated for both the Point and TextField objects.

13. The object reference, hvy, refers to the newly created Heavy object on the heap.

As you can see, creating heavyweight objects is much less efficient than creating lightweight objects. Step 12 is the most costly because it must repeat the entire process for both aggregate objects. Objects of the Light class are more than five times faster to create than objects of the Heavy class.

If you determine through profiling that a performance problem is due to the creation of heavyweight objects, you have a few options:

- Use lazy evaluation techniques (see PRAXIS 43).

- Redesign the class to make it lighter.

- If the code that causes the performance problem uses only part of the heavyweight object, break up the heavyweight class into multiple lightweight classes. This enables the performance-critical code to access only objects of the lightweight classes.

Given the performance implications of heavyweight objects, you might decide not to design heavyweight classes. This is unwise. Not all objects in a design can be lightweight. Heavyweight objects have valid uses and including them in a design is fine. The goal is not to avoid heavyweight objects but rather to understand their performance implications as you work on performance improvements.

When working on performance improvements, keep in mind that the following class attributes increase the time it takes to create an object of that class:

- Large amounts of code in the constructor

- Containment of many objects, or large objects, that are initialized as part of the constructor

- Deep inheritance hierarchy, for example if the class's base class is not its immediate superclass

Also, keep in mind that each object created is another one for the garbage collector to keep track of and potentially free. Therefore, not only is there a cost to object creation, but also a cost for the garbage collector to appropriately manage the storage. An alternative to creating new objects is to reuse existing ones (see PRAXIS 42).

PRAXIS 33: **Guard against unused objects**

PRAXIS 32 discusses the high cost of object creation. This high cost means that objects should be created only when they are needed. Careless coding practices lead to the unnecessary creation of objects, and this slows down code execution. For example, consider a method that takes two arrays as input, adds their contents, stores the results in another array, and returns the created array. This code might look like this:

```
//...
public final static int ArraySize = 10;
//...
public int[] addArrays(int[] arr1, int[] arr2)
{
```

114

```
    int[] result = new int[ArraySize];
    IllegalArgumentException exc = new IllegalArgumentException
                                    ("arrays are invalid");

    if (arr1 != null && arr2 != null &&
        arr1.length == ArraySize && arr2.length == ArraySize)
    {
      for (int i=0; i<ArraySize; i++)
        result[i] = arr1[i] + arr2[i];
    }
    else
      throw exc;
    return result;
}
```

This code is inefficient because it always creates an object that is not used. The
code initially creates an array object and an exception object. However, only one
of these objects is used during the execution of the method. Because of the way
the method is implemented, there is no way for both of these objects to be used.
This implementation means that you always pay for two objects to be created, one
of which is completely useless depending on the path taken through the code.

Here is a better way to write this method:

```
//...
public final static int ArraySize = 10;
//...
public int[] addArrays(int[] arr1, int[] arr2)
{
  if (arr1 != null && arr2 != null &&
      arr1.length == ArraySize && arr2.length == ArraySize)
  {
    int[] result = new int[ArraySize];
    for (int i=0; i<ArraySize; i++)
      result[i] = arr1[i] + arr2[i];
    return result;
  }
  throw new IllegalArgumentException("arrays are invalid");
}
```

This method is more efficient because it creates only the objects that it uses—the
array and exception objects—and only when they are needed. Therefore, only one
object is ever created when this method is called. This modified method is more
than five times faster than the original method when provided with valid input
arrays.

Object creation is very expensive. Be absolutely certain not to create unnecessary objects.

PRAXIS 34: **Minimize synchronization**

When writing multithreaded code, you will come across many instances in which the `synchronized` keyword is used to limit access to shared resources (see PRAXES 46 and 47). The `synchronized` keyword is useful and necessary. However, a cost is associated with its use that you must understand when designing classes. For example, consider the following class that implements a stack:

```java
class Stack
{
  private int[] intArr;
  private int index;

  Stack(int v)
  {
    intArr = new int[v];
  }

  public int top()
  {
    return intArr[0];
  }

  public void push(int val)
  {
    intArr[index] = val;
    index++;
  }

  public int pop()
  {
    index--;
    return intArr[index];
  }

  public boolean contains(int val)
  {
    int size = intArr.length;
    boolean found = false;
    for (int i=0; i<size; i++)
    {
      if (intArr[i] == val)
      {
        found = true;
```

```
            break;
        }
    }
    return found;
    }
}
```

Currently, none of the methods are synchronized. Assume that an object of the Stack class needs to be accessed by multiple threads. You correctly change each method to be synchronized. What is the performance effect of this change? How do the synchronized methods perform relative to the non-synchronized methods?

The synchronized versions of the push, pop, and top methods are about five to six times slower than their non-synchronized versions. However, the synchronized contains method is only 10 percent slower than its non-synchronized version. This raises two questions:

1. Why is there such a large difference between the execution times of the synchronized and non-synchronized versions of the push, pop, and top methods?

2. Why is there a small difference between the execution times of the synchronized and non-synchronized contains method?

Focusing on the method top, you might look to the generated bytecode for a clue as to why the synchronized version is so much slower than the non-synchronized version. Ironically, the generated bytecode for these two methods is identical:

```
Method int top()
    0 aload_0          //Push the object reference(this) at index
                       //0 of the local variable table.
    1 getfield #6 <Field int intArr[]>
                       //Pop the object reference(this) and push
                       //the object reference for intArr accessed
                       //from the constant pool.
    4 iconst_0         //Push 0.
    5 iaload           //Pop the top two values and push the value
                       //at index 0 of intArr.
    6 ireturn          //Pop the top value and push it onto the
                       //operand stack of the invoker.
```

If their bytecode is the same, how can one be five to six times faster than the other?

When the synchronized method modifier is present, as in the synchronized version of method top, the acquisition and subsequent release of the lock is not done with the monitorenter and monitorexit opcodes. Instead, when the JVM invokes a method it checks for the ACC_SYNCHRONIZED property flag.[8] If this flag is present, then the thread that is executing acquires a lock, calls the method, and then releases the lock when the method returns. If an exception is thrown from a synchronized method, the lock is automatically released before the exception leaves the method.

The synchronized method top is so much slower than the non-synchronized version because of the cost to acquire and release the lock. For a small method, this cost makes up a large percentage of the total runtime of the method.

By contrast, the synchronized contains method is only about 10 percent slower than the non-synchronized version. It still must acquire and release the lock. However, it has more code than the push, pop, or top methods. The cost to acquire the lock is amortized across the longer runtime of a larger method. Therefore, for a larger method, the cost to acquire the lock is a smaller percentage of the method's total runtime.

The synchronized keyword not only slows down code, it also can make code larger depending on how it is used. For example, the following two methods are functionally equivalent:

```
public synchronized int top1()
{
  return intArr[0];
}

public int top2()
{
  synchronized (this) {
    return intArr[0];
  }
}
```

[8.] The ACC_SYNCHRONIZED property flag is included in a method's method_info structure if the synchronized method modifier is present.

These methods are functionally identical. What is not obvious, however, is that they have different performance and size characteristics. In this case, `top1` is approximately 13 percent faster than `top2` as well as much smaller. Examine the generated bytecode to see how these methods differ:

```
Method int top1()
    0 aload_0          //Push the object reference(this) at index
                       //0 of the local variable table.
    1 getfield #6 <Field int intArr[]>
                       //Pop the object reference(this) and push
                       //the object reference for intArr accessed
                       //from the constant pool.
    4 iconst_0         //Push 0.
    5 iaload           //Pop the top two values and push the value
                       //at index 0 of intArr.
    6 ireturn          //Pop top value and push it on the operand
                       //stack of the invoking method. Exit method.

Method int top2()
    0 aload_0          //Push the object reference(this) at index
                       //0 of the local variable table.
    1 astore_2         //Pop the object reference(this) and store
                       //it at index 2 of the local variable table.
    2 aload_2          //Push the object reference(this).
    3 monitorenter     //Pop the object reference(this) and acquire
                       //the object's monitor.
    4 aload_0          //Beginning of the synchronized block. Push
                       //the object reference(this) at index 0 of
                       //the local variable table.
    5 getfield #6 <Field int intArr[]>
                       //Pop the object reference(this) and push
                       //the object reference for intArr accessed
                       //from the constant pool.
    8 iconst_0         //Push 0.
    9 iaload           //Pop the top two values and push the value
                       //at index 0 of intArr.
   10 istore_1         //Pop the value and store it at index 1 of
                       //the local variable table.
   11 jsr 19           //Push the address of the next opcode(14)
                       //and jump to location 19.
   14 iload_1          //Push the value at index 1 of the local
                       //variable table.
   15 ireturn          //Pop top value and push it on the operand
                       //stack of the invoking method. Exit method.
   16 aload_2          //End of the synchronized block. Push the
                       //object reference(this) at index 2 of the
                       //local variable table.
   17 monitorexit      //Pop the object reference(this) and exit
                       //the monitor.
```

```
18 athrow              //Pop the object reference(this) and throw
                       //an exception.
19 astore_3            //Pop the return address(14) and store it at
                       //index 3 of the local variable table.
20 aload_2             //Push the object reference(this) at index 2
                       //of the local variable table.
21 monitorexit         //Pop the object reference(this) and exit
                       //the monitor.
22 ret 3               //Return to the location indicated by index
                       //3 of the local variable table(14).
Exception table:       //If any exception occurs between
from   to   target type //location 4 (inclusive) and location
 4     16    16    any //16 (exclusive) jump to location 16.
```

top2 is larger and slower than top1 because of how the synchronization and exception processing is done. Remember, `top1` uses the `synchronized` method modifier, which does not generate extra code. By contrast, `top2` uses a `synchronized` statement in the body of the method.

Using `synchronized` in the body of the method generates the bytecode for the `monitorenter` and `monitorexit` opcodes, as well as additional code to handle exceptions. If an exception is generated while executing inside of a `synchronized` block (a monitor), the lock is guaranteed to be released prior to exiting the `synchronized` block. The implementation of `top1` is slightly more efficient than that of `top2`—this results in a very small performance gain.

Therefore, the limitation of synchronization has positive performance benefits. (See PRAXIS 49 for techniques to avoid unnecessary synchronization.) Unfortunately, synchronization is not always easy to eliminate. Sometimes you use `synchronized` methods provided by a class library even though you do not need synchronization. For example, you might write a single-threaded application but call `synchronized` methods of a library that are designed for multithreaded access. In this case, you still pay the large cost of a `synchronized` method to acquire and release a lock you do not need. To eliminate this type of unnecessary `synchronization`, you have two options:

1. Provide a subclass that contains unsynchronized versions of the same methods.

2. Use an alternative class that provides unsynchronized methods.

Option 1 works only if you have access to the source code for the `synchronized` methods you want to replace. For example, consider the following classes:

```
class Stack
{ //As before...
  public synchronized int top()
  {
    return intArr[0];
  }
}
class UnsyncStack extends Stack
{
  public int top()
  {
    return intArr[0];
  }
  //...
}
```

This code simply provides a subclass with an unsynchronized version of the method that you want to use. The disadvantages of this technique are an increased amount of code and a performance penalty associated with using a more heavy-weight object. (For more on heavyweight objects, see PRAXIS 32.) Furthermore, because you duplicate code, there is more to maintain, as well as an increase in the .class file size and memory usage for your program.

When you do not have access to the source code or cannot afford the extra size or memory overhead, you are left with option 2. One case in which this option can be used is with the Vector class. The Vector class is very useful to store and manipulate objects. It differs from an array in various features (see PRAXIS 4). However, most of its methods are synchronized. Therefore, when you do not need the synchronized semantics, you still pay the performance penalty associated with them. This makes using a Vector in these cases less than optimal.

Prior to the Java 2 SDK, programmers used option 1 and implemented an unsynchronized Vector. They did this by creating a subclass of the java.util.Vector class and providing versions of the methods they used, but without the synchronized keyword. This technique is no longer necessary with the ArrayList class introduced in the Java 2 collection classes. The ArrayList class is essentially an unsynchronized Vector and as a result is much faster. For example, consider the following code that uses a Vector:

```
Vector v = new Vector(10);
for (int i=0; i<10; i++)
{
  Button b = new Button("button text");
  v.add(b);
}
```

This code can be easily replaced with an `ArrayList` class, as follows:

```
ArrayList al = new ArrayList(10);
for (int i=0; i<10; i++)
{
  Button b = new Button("button text");
  al.add(b);
}
```

The `ArrayList` implementation of this code is more than twice as fast as that of the `Vector` and yields the same results. Keep in mind that the unsynchronized version of the `ArrayList` class should be used only when synchronization is not needed.

Declaring `synchronized` methods or methods that have `synchronized` blocks can decrease performance drastically. Furthermore, whether you use `synchronized` as a method modifier or with the `synchronized` block, there are size implications. Use `synchronized` methods only when your code requires synchronization and you understand the cost imposed by their usage. If an entire method needs to be `synchronized`, prefer the method modifier over the `synchronized` block in order to produce smaller and slightly faster code.

PRAXIS 35: Use stack variables whenever possible

When frequently accessing variables, you need to consider from where they are accessed. Is the variable `static`, on the stack, or an instance variable of a class? Where you store a variable has a significant impact on the performance of code that accesses it. For example, consider the following code:

```
class StackVars
{
  private int instVar;
  private static int staticVar;

  //Stack variable access
  void stackAccess(int val)
  {
    int j=0;
    for (int i=0; i<val; i++)
      j += 1;
  }
```

```
  //Class instance variable access
  void instanceAccess(int val)
  {
    for (int i=0; i<val; i++)
      instVar += 1;
  }

  //Class static variable access
  void staticAccess(int val)
  {
    for (int i=0; i<val; i++)
      staticVar += 1;
  }
}
```

Each method in this code executes the same loop for the same number of iterations. They differ only in that each loop increments a different type of variable. The method stackAccess increments a local stack variable, instanceAccess increments a class instance variable, and staticAccess increments a class static variable.

instanceAccess and staticAccess take about the same amount of time to execute. stackAccess, however, is two to three times faster. Accessing a stack variable is so much faster because the JVM performs less work than when accessing static or class instance variables. Look at the generated bytecode for the three methods:

```
Method void stackAccess(int)
     0 iconst_0        //Push 0 onto the stack.
     1 istore_2        //Pop 0 and store it at index 2 of the local
                       //variable table(j).
     2 iconst_0        //Push 0.
     3 istore_3        //Pop 0 and store it at index 3 of the local
                       //variable table(i).
     4 goto 13         //Jump to location 13.
     7 iinc 2 1        //Increment j stored at index 2 by 1.
    10 iinc 3 1        //Increment i stored at index 3 by 1.
    13 iload_3         //Push the value at index 3(i).
    14 iload_1         //Push the value at index 1(val).
    15 if_icmplt 7     //Pop i and val. Jump to location 7 if i is
                       //less than val.
    18 return          //Return to calling method.

Method void instanceAccess(int)
     0 iconst_0        //Push 0 onto the stack.
     1 istore_2        //Pop 0 and store it at index 2 of the local
                       //variable table(i).
```

```
  2 goto 18           //Jump to location 18.
  5 aload_0           //Push index 0(this).
  6 dup               //Duplicate the top stack value and push it.
  7 getfield #19 <Field int instVar>
                      //Pop the object reference for this and push
                      //the value for instVar.
 10 iconst_1          //Push 1.
 11 iadd              //Pop the top two values, push their sum.
 12 putfield #19 <Field int instVar>
                      //Pop the top two values and store the sum
                      //in instVar.
 15 iinc 2 1          //Increment i stored at index 2 by 1.
 18 iload_2           //Push the value at index 2(i).
 19 iload_1           //Push the value at index 1(val).
 20 if_icmplt 5       //Pop i and val. Jump to location 5 if i is
                      //less than val.
 23 return            //Return to calling method.

Method void staticAccess(int)
  0 iconst_0          //Push 0 onto the stack.
  1 istore_2          //Pop 0 and store it at index 2 of the local
                      //variable table(i).
  2 goto 16           //Jump to location 16.
  5 getstatic #25 <Field int staticVar>
                      //Push the value from the constant pool for
                      //staticVar.
  8 iconst_1          //Push 1.
  9 iadd              //Pop the top two values, push their sum.
 10 putstatic #25 <Field int staticVar>
                      //Pop the value for sum and store it in
                      //staticVar.
 13 iinc 2 1          //Increment i stored at index 2 by 1.
 16 iload_2           //Push the value at index 2(i).
 17 iload_1           //Push the value at index 1(val).
 18 if_icmplt 5       //Pop i and val. Jump to location 5 if i is
                      //less than val.
 21 return            //Return to calling method.
```

Looking at the bytecode reveals why stack variables are more efficient. The JVM is a stack-based machine and therefore is optimized to access and manipulate stack data. All local variables are stored in a local variable table and manipulated on the Java operand stack and can be accessed very efficiently. Accessing `static` and instance variables is more costly because the JVM must use a more expensive opcode and access them from the constant pool.[9]

---

9. The constant pool holds symbolic references to all types, fields, and methods used by a type.

Typically, after the first access of a static or instance variable from the constant pool, the bytecode is dynamically changed by the JVM to use a more efficient opcode. Regardless of this optimization, stack variables are still faster to access.

Given these facts, the previous code can be restructured to operate more efficiently by accessing stack variables instead of instance or static variables. Consider the modified code:

```
class StackVars
{
  //As before...

  void instanceAccess(int val)
  {
    int j = instVar;

    for (int i=0; i<val; i++)
      j += 1;
    instVar = j;
  }

  void staticAccess(int val)
  {
    int j = staticVar;
    for (int i=0; i<val; i++)
      j += 1;
    staticVar = j;
  }
}
```

The methods instanceAccess and staticAccess are modified to copy their instance or static variables to a local stack variable. When manipulation of a variable is complete, the value is copied back to the instance or static variable. This simple change significantly improves the performance of instanceAccess and staticAccess. The execution times of the three methods are now effectively equal, with instanceAccess and staticAccess executing only about 4 percent slower than stackAccess.

This does not mean you should avoid using static or instance variables. You should use whatever storage mechanism makes sense for your design. For example, if you access static or instance variables in a loop, you can significantly improve the performance of the code by temporarily storing them in a local stack variable. This provides a more efficient sequence of bytecode instructions for the JVM to execute.

PRAXIS 36: Use `static`, `final`, and `private` methods to allow inlining

For a method to be considered a candidate for inlining, it must be declared `private`, `static`, or `final`. Methods of these types can be statically resolved at compile time and, therefore, do not require dynamic resolution.

Replacing a method call with the method body leads to faster code. Typically, only small methods are considered for inlining due to increased code problems encountered with inlining large methods. Methods that are usually inlined include the simple getters and setters common in a class. These methods are normally only one or two lines long. For example, consider the following code:

```java
class Test
{
  private int len;
  public int length()
  {
    return len;
  }
  public void setLength(int val)
  {
    len = val;
  }
  //...
}
```

Assuming that a Java compiler or a JIT has the capability to inline methods, these methods will be inlined in each method that invokes them if they are declared `static`, `final`, or `private`. This will improve their performance without significantly increasing their size. For example, the previous code could be modified as follows to enable method inlining:

```java
class Test
{
  private int len;
  public final int length()
  {
    return len;
  }
  public final void setLength(int val)
  {
    len = val;
  }
  //...
}
```

These methods are not inlined by most existing Java compilers. They will, however, be inlined at runtime by most JITs. The inlining of these methods usually results in a significant performance gain. For example, the inlined implementations of the `length` and `setLength` methods are more than three times faster than the non-inlined implementations. Similar performance improvements are seen when the methods are made `static` or `private`, as this enables inlining in the same way that `final` does.

Declaring methods as `static`, `final`, or `private` has the drawback that such methods cannot be extended with subclassing. This restricts what a derived class can do with the methods of a class.

Noticeable performance improvements are achieved only when the method is called many times. This is because when a method is inlined, you do not have the overhead of the method call. The more times a method is called, the more savings are generated. However, inlining might cause your code to grow. If the method has many call sites, the size of the `.class` file can grow because the code that is normally stored once is duplicated in all places from which it was previously called.

The decision to inline a method can be made either by the compiler at compile time or by the JIT at runtime. Different Java compilers and JITs might use different rules to decide whether to inline a method. Certain compilers might also have an option to disable inlining.

There are advantages and disadvantages to having the compiler, rather than the JIT, perform inlining. When the compiler inlines a method, the JIT has less work to do, and thus the runtime of your code is that much more efficient. However, with compiler inlining any changes to that method are not used by other code in other `.class` files unless the code is recompiled. By contrast, when the method is inlined at runtime by the JIT, a new implementation of the method is used by other classes on subsequent program invocations.

PRAXIS 37:   Initialize instance variables only once

A large percentage of program execution time for object-oriented systems is spent creating and destroying objects. PRAXIS 32 discusses the high cost of object creation. Because the creation of an object invokes a constructor on the class, it is advantageous for the constructor to be as efficient as possible.

You can make constructors more efficient by having them do less work. To accomplish this safely, you must know exactly what is happening when an object is created. PRAXIS 32 details the steps necessary to create and initialize an object. This PRAXIS shows how to make that process more efficient.

Consider the following class definition and its constructor implementation:

```
class Foo
{
  private int count;
  private boolean done;
  private Point pt;
  private Vector vec;

  public Foo()
  {
    count = 0;                                                    //1
    done = false;
    pt = new Point(0,0);
    vec = new Vector(10);
  }
}
```

Notice that the count and done fields are initialized in the body of the constructor. You might also see this class implemented as follows:

```
class Foo2
{
  private int count = 0;
  private boolean done = false;
  private Point pt;
  private Vector vec;

  public Foo2()
  {
    pt = new Point(0,0);
    vec = new Vector(10);
  }
}
```

Both of the class implementations here are inefficient. PRAXIS 32 shows that when an object of a class is created, the instance variables of the class are initialized to their default values based on their types. Then, before the body of the constructor executes, instance variable initialization is done. Finally, the body of the constructor executes. Both of these class implementations initialize the count and done variables twice to the same value.

When the body of the constructor for class Foo is entered, the instance variables count, done, pt, and vec have already been assigned their default values, to 0, false, null, and null, respectively. The body of the constructor then unnecessarily reinitializes count and done to 0 and false, respectively.

For class Foo2, the four instance variables have been set to their default values. Then, before the constructor executes, the instance variable initialization is performed, resetting count and done to their default values.

Because these two instance variables were initialized to their default values by the JVM when the object was allocated, their default values need not be reset in the body of the constructor or during instance variable initialization. A more efficient implementation of these classes looks like this:

```
class Foo
{
  private int count;
  private boolean done;
  private Point pt;
  private Vector vec;

  public Foo()
  {
    pt = new Point(0,0);
    vec = new Vector(10);
  }
}
```

Granted, this is only a small savings of a few bytecode instructions. Nevertheless, these savings add up for an object that is constructed repeatedly. Furthermore, less code is generated for this implementation. The .class file no longer contains unnecessary code to assign count the value 0 and done the value false. count and done are initialized to their default values by the JVM, not by the constructor or instance variable initialization. This version of the class is the smallest and fastest of the three versions. An optimizing compiler should eliminate these extraneous assignments. Unfortunately, many compilers do not (see PRAXIS 29).

Many programmers familiar with other programming languages are uncomfortable not explicitly initializing all instance data. Some languages do not provide default initial values for data as a performance tuning feature. Programmers usually initialize data before it is accessed. Therefore, for some, the previous class implementation might look a bit strange at first glance.

Because Java performs default initialization for instance variables, static variables, and arrays, this performance effect need not be further negated by needless initialization of these variables and arrays to their default values. Keep in mind that local variables do not have a default value and thus must be explicitly initialized. Only static and instance variables of a class have default values. These are given in Table 1 on page 8. (This table also shows the default values for arrays based on type.)

PRAXIS 38: Use primitive types for faster and smaller code

Java provides several primitive types, as well as an associated primitive wrapper class for each. Primitive types and objects have different storage and behavioral characteristics, which are outlined in PRAXIS 8. Not only do primitive types behave differently and have different storage characteristics, they also exhibit different performance and size characteristics. Each primitive type and its associated wrapper class is shown in Table 3 on page 25.

The storage required to represent a primitive type is typically no larger than the amount of storage required to hold its range of values. For a 32-bit machine architecture, this size is typically 4 or 8 bytes. (For the remainder of this discussion, a 32-bit machine is assumed.) Therefore, storing all primitive types takes a maximum of 4 bytes each, with the exception of double and long, which each take a maximum of 8 bytes. The smaller primitive types (short, byte, char, and boolean) are often represented more compactly when used in fields of objects or classes or as array elements. They are, however, typically promoted to an int and use 4 bytes of storage when stored on the stack or used in local variables.

In addition to being small, primitive types are also fast to access. Primitive types do not have an object associated with them. Their values, therefore, are stored directly on the stack. Creating them is fast because the JVM must reserve only 4 bytes (8 bytes in the case of double and long) on the stack for their storage. Access to primitive types is also fast because they are accessed directly with specific opcode instructions.

Objects, on the other hand, are larger and more expensive to access than primitive types. An object's exact representation on the heap in the JVM is implementation-dependent. Whatever its exact representation, an object needs additional storage in order to have access to class-specific data. For example, an object might store a pointer to its instance data and another to its class-specific data. This results in an immediate overhead of 8 bytes (4 bytes for each pointer).

In addition to the size overhead of objects, they are more expensive than primitive types to access. This is because of the indirection involved. Consider the following method with a primitive `int` and a reference to an `Integer` object on the stack. The following diagram shows a possible representation of the stack, heap, and object layout for this code:[10]

```
public void foo()
{
   int i = 5;
   Integer iobj = new Integer(10);
   bar(iobj.intValue());
   //...
}
```

With this implementation, the primitive `int` is accessed quickly with direct access to the stack. Accessing the object, however, requires indirection to get to the heap where it is located. Instance data can then be accessed directly. Access to methods requires another indirect pointer access.

Because of these characteristics, you use less memory and your code executes faster if you use the primitive types rather than their wrappers. Consider the following two methods:

```
public int usePrimitive(int increment)
{
   int i = 5;
   i = i + increment;
   return i;
}
public int useObject(Integer increment)
{
   int i = 5;
   i = i + increment.intValue();
   return i;
}
```

---

10. The exact representation of the object is implementation-dependent. One possible implementation is shown.

Both methods simply add two numbers together and return the result. The use-Primitive method uses two primitive int types, and the useObject method uses one primitive int and one Integer wrapper class.

You might think that using only one primitive wrapper class does not affect code performance. The results say otherwise. The usePrimitive method is about 30 percent faster than the useObject method. To understand why using the Integer class is slower, examine the generated bytecode for these two methods. The usePrimitive method generates the following bytecode:

```
Method int usePrimitive(int)
   0 iconst_5      //Push 5 on the stack.
   1 istore_2      //Pop 5 and store it at index 2 of the local
                   //variable table(i).
   2 iload_2       //Push the value from index 2 of the local
                   //variable table(i).
   3 iload_1       //Push the value from index 1 of the local
                   //variable table(increment).
   4 iadd          //Pop the top two values, push their sum.
   5 istore_2      //Pop the sum and store it at index 2 of the
                   //local variable table(i).
   6 iload_2       //Push the value from index 2 of the local
                   //variable table(i).
   7 ireturn       //Pop the top value and push it on the operand
                   //stack of the invoking method.
```

Assuming you pass the value 10, this code simply pushes the values 5 and 10 onto the stack, adds them, and returns the result.

Compare the usePrimitive method bytecode with the generated bytecode for the useObject method:

```
Method int useObject(java.lang.Integer)
   0 iconst_5      //Push 5 on the stack.
   1 istore_2      //Pop 5 and store it at index 2 of the local
                   //variable table(i).
   2 iload_2       //Push the value from index 2 of the local
                   //variable table(i).
   3 aload_1       //Push the object reference from index 1 of the
                   //local variable table(increment).
   4 invokevirtual #16 <Method int intValue()>
                   //Pop the object reference and invoke its
                   //intValue method. Push the result.
   7 iadd          //Pop the two top values, push their sum.
   8 istore_2      //Pop the sum and store it at index 2 of the
                   //local variable table(i).
   9 iload_2       //Push the value from index 2(i).
```

```
10 ireturn          //Pop the top value and push it on the operand
                    //stack of the invoking method.
```

Because this method is passed an `Integer` object, the `intValue` method of the `Integer` class is called to retrieve the value stored in it. Not only do you incur a method call, but you also pay the additional costs associated with accessing an object rather than a primitive type. These differences account for the variance in the runtime between the two methods.

You also should be aware of the situation in which a method constructs a primitive wrapper object to satisfy its return value. For example, consider the modified `useObject` method, which is passed the value `10`, that returns an `Integer` object instead of an `int`:

```
public Integer useObject(int increment)
{
  int i = 5;
  i = i + increment;
  return (new Integer(i));
}
```

This code is much slower and larger than either of the first two examples. The dramatic slowdown results because each time the method is called, an object is created. Object creation is slow and, if possible, should be minimized in order to enhance performance (see PRAXIS 32).

The code is also larger due to the extra bytecode necessary to create the object. This method generates the following bytecode:

```
Method java.lang.Integer useObject(int)
    0 iconst_5        //Push 5 on the stack.
    1 istore_2        //Pop 5 and store it at index 2 of the local
                      //variable table(i).
    2 iload_2         //Push the value from index 2 of the local
                      //variable table(i).
    3 iload_1         //Push the value from index 1 of the local
                      //variable table(increment).
    4 iadd            //Pop the two top values and push their sum.
    5 istore_2        //Pop the sum and store it at index 2 of the
                      //local variable table(i).
    6 new #4 <Class java.lang.Integer>
                      //Create an object of the Integer class and
                      //push a reference to it.
    9 dup             //Duplicate the top stack value and push it.
   10 iload_2         //Push the value from index 2 of the local
                      //variable table(i).
```

```
11 invokespecial #11 <Method java.lang.Integer(int)>
                   //Pop the top two values and invoke the
                   //constructor for the Integer class passing i.
14 areturn         //Pop the object reference for the Integer
                   //object and push it on the operand stack of
                   //the invoking method.
```

A more efficient implementation of this method would be to change its return value to an `int` and avoid the creation of the object.

As a result of this, you might think that there is absolutely no use for the primitive wrapper classes. In addition, based on the performance and size differences between primitive types and their wrappers, you might not want to use them. However, sometimes you need to use them. All of the collection classes in Java operate on objects of type `java.lang.Object`. This means that if you try to add a primitive type to a collection, you get a compiler error. To resolve the compiler error, you must wrap the primitive with its wrapper class. For example:

```
Vector v = new Vector();
v.add(5);   //ERROR
v.add(new Integer(5));   //OK
```

When using collections, you have no choice but to use objects. Alternatively, you might want to use the primitive wrappers exclusively. You might want the additional behavior of the wrapper classes and are willing to trade some performance for a better design. Using only the primitive wrappers is fine as long as you understand the size and speed implications associated with their use. In other code, however, using these wrapper classes less often yields smaller and faster code.

Some object-oriented purists disagree with the decision of the Java designers to include primitive types. They argue that if Java was truly object-oriented, it would have only objects and no primitive types. Regardless of the merits of these arguments, the fact is, the language has both. Java programmers can take advantage of the speed and size characteristics of primitive types when the performance of a system requires it.

PRAXIS 39:   **Do not use an Enumeration or an Iterator to traverse a Vector**

Four ways are available to traverse the elements of a Vector in Java:

1. Iterator

2. ListIterator

3. Enumeration

4. The get method

Consider a method that traverses a Vector of Integer objects. The sum of the values of all Integer objects is computed and returned. This method can be written in four different ways, as follows:

```java
public int enumVec(Vector vec)
{
  Enumeration enum = vec.elements();
  int total = 0;
  while(enum.hasMoreElements())
    total += ((Integer)(enum.nextElement())).intValue();
  return total;
}

public int iterVec(Vector vec)
{
  Iterator iter = vec.iterator();
  int total = 0;
  while(iter.hasNext())
    total += ((Integer)(iter.next())).intValue();
  return total;
}

public int listIterVec(Vector vec)
{
  ListIterator iter = vec.listIterator();
  int total = 0;
  while(iter.hasNext())
    total += ((Integer)(iter.next())).intValue();
  return total;
}

public int forVec(Vector vec)
{
  int size = vec.size();
  int total = 0;
```

```
    for (int i=0; i<size; i++)
      total += ((Integer)(vec.get(i))).intValue();
    return total;
}
```

All four of these methods perform the same task and return the same result, given the same input Vector. Three methods, however, have different performance characteristics from each other. The performance of the Iterator and ListIterator are roughly the same. The Enumeration is about 12 percent faster. However, a standard for loop with the Vector class's get method results in code that is between 29 percent and 34 percent faster than the other three methods.

The forVec method is faster than the others because it does less work. Notice that each time through the loop, forVec makes two method calls, one each to get and intValue. By contrast, all of the other methods make three method calls for each loop iteration. For example, the enumVec method calls hasMoreElements, next-Element, and intValue.

The extra method call each time through the loop makes these enumerations and iterators slower than get and a for loop. In time-critical code, consider replacing these more expensive constructs with cheaper ones.

PRAXIS 40: Use System.arraycopy for copying arrays

Other PRAXES in this section discuss the high cost of method calls and the need to eliminate them where possible. As with anything else, there are exceptions. For example, programmers might write code to copy one array to another with a standard for loop construct like this:

```
int[] src;
int[] dest;
//Assumes src and dest have same length...
int size = src.length;
for (int i=0; i<size; i++)
  dest[i] = src[i];
```

You might think this is the most efficient way to copy arrays in Java. There is, however, a more efficient technique. The System class of the java.lang package contains the following method:

```
public static native void arraycopy(Object src, int src_position,
                    Object dst, int dst_position, int length);
```

This method takes a source array and a destination array, starting positions for each, and a length. Note that the source and destination parameters are of type Object. You must ensure that you pass this method two array objects and a valid length in order to avoid an exception. Using System.arraycopy as a replacement for a for loop results in faster code.

Consider two methods for copying arrays. One is implemented with a for loop and the other with System.arraycopy. Their implementations looks like this:

```
public void copyArray1(int[] src, int[] dest)
{
  int size = src.length;  //Assumes src and dest have same length
  for (int i=0; i<size; i++)
    dest[i] = src[i];
}

public void copyArray2(int[] src, int[] dest)
{
  int size = src.length;  //Assumes src and dest have same length
  System.arraycopy(src, 0, dest, 0, size);
}
```

Using System.arraycopy to copy arrays is more than twice as fast as using the for loop. You might wonder how a method call can be faster than inline code. First, look at the generated bytecode for the two methods:

```
Method void copyArray1(int[], int[])
    0 aload_1          //Push the object reference at index 1 of
                       //the local variable table(src).
    1 arraylength      //Pop src and push its length.
    2 istore_3         //Pop the length and store it at index 3 of
                       //the local variable table(size).
    3 iconst_0         //Push 0.
    4 istore 4         //Pop 0 and store it at index 4 of the local
                       //variable table(i).
    6 goto 20          //Jump to location 20.
    9 aload_2          //Push the object reference at index 2 of
                       //the local variable table(dest).
   10 iload 4          //Push the value at index 4(i).
   12 aload_1          //Push the object reference at index 1 of
                       //the local variable table(src).
   13 iload 4          //Push the value at index 4(i).
   15 iaload           //Pop i and src. Push the ith element of the
                       //src array.
   16 iastore          //Pop the top three values (ith element of
                       //src, i, and dest). Store the ith element
                       //or src at index i of dest.
```

```
 17 iinc 4 1          //Increment i stored at index 4.
 20 iload 4           //Push the value at index 4(i).
 22 iload_3           //Push the value at index 3(size).
 23 if_icmplt 9       //Pop i and size. Jump to location 9 if i is
                      //less than size.
 26 return            //Return to calling method.

Method void copyArray2(int[], int[])
  0 aload_1           //Push the object reference at index 1 of
                      //the local variable table(src).
  1 arraylength       //Pop src and push its length.
  2 istore_3          //Pop the length and store it at index 3 of
                      //the local variable table(size).
  3 aload_1           //Push the object reference at index 1 of
                      //the local variable table(src).
  4 iconst_0          //Push 0.
  5 aload_2           //Push the object reference at index 2 of
                      //the local variable table(dest).
  6 iconst_0          //Push 0.
  7 iload_3           //Push the value at index 3(size).
  8 invokestatic #13  <Method void arraycopy(java.lang.Object,
                      int, java.lang.Object, int, int)>
                      //Pop the top five values and call the
                      //arraycopy method.
 11 return            //Return to calling method.
```

A quick look at the bytecode reveals what we expect. The copyArray2 method is smaller than copyArray1. After all, it makes a method call to do the work, instead of performing it inline. The copyArray2 method is faster because the method it calls, System.arraycopy, is implemented as a native method. Because it is implemented natively, the method can directly, and efficiently, move the memory of the source array to the destination array. This operation can absorb the cost of the native method call and still perform significantly faster than plain Java code. Because it is a native method, the speed of this call on various platforms will vary.

PRAXIS 41: Prefer an array to a Vector or ArrayList

The Java 2 SDK provides various collection classes to store objects. The Java Vector class is one such collection. Many programmers default to using the Vector for simple collections because it is very convenient and simple to use. An array, by contrast, differs from a Vector in various ways (see PRAXIS 4). One key way they differ is in their performance characteristics. Consider the following code that utilizes an array and a Vector:

```
public void iterateArray(int[] ar)
{
  int size = ar.length;
  int j;
  for (int i=0; i<size; i++)
    j = ar[i];
}
public void iterateVector(Vector vec)
{
  int size = vec.size();
  Object j;
  for (int i=0; i<size; i++)
    j = vec.get(i);
}
```

Notice that this code simply iterates over the given array or Vector. Nothing is done with the data stored in either. This is simply an exercise in how fast arrays are accessed compared to a Vector. You might have figured out that the array implementation is faster, but you might not have realized how much faster. The iterateArray method is more than 40 times faster than the iterateVector method. iterateVector is even slower if it uses an Enumeration or an Iterator to traverse itself (see PRAXIS 39).

The large performance difference between an array and a Vector occurs because:

1. The get method of Vector is synchronized (see PRAXIS 34).

2. Using the Vector requires method calls (see PRAXIS 38).

The array implementation does not suffer from either of these conditions. In addition, as discussed in PRAXIS 4, the Java Vector class is implemented in terms of an array. Therefore, whenever you create a Vector, the code creates an array for the storage and management of the objects it contains.

Another class you might consider using in place of the Vector is ArrayList. This class essentially is an unsynchronized Vector and as a result is much faster than the Vector. The previous code, modified with an ArrayList, looks like this:

```
public void iterateArrayList(ArrayList al)
{
  int size = al.size();
  Object j;
  for (int i=0; i<size; i++)
    j = al.get(i);
}
```

This code is almost four times faster than the Vector. However, the array is still 11 times faster than the ArrayList.

Given this, should you ever use anything but an array? The Vector and Array-List are very useful because they automatically resize themselves when more objects are added than their current size can accommodate. However, you pay a high price for this feature. Both the Vector and ArrayList classes are implemented in terms of an array. Therefore, when these classes resize themselves, a new array is created and everything is copied from the old array to the new array. The object that originally would not fit is then added.

The Vector and ArrayList have another side effect that might not be obvious. Whenever an element is removed from them, each of the other items at an index greater than the element removed is moved to have an index one less than it had before the removal. This is done so no "holes" are left in the underlying array. Unfortunately, this operation can be expensive.

Because of these properties of the Vector and ArrayList, removing an element from the beginning of them is expensive. The farther toward the end that the element is when it is removed, the faster this operation is. Furthermore, the entire array for the Vector or ArrayList is copied when an element is added for which there is no room. The larger the Vector or ArrayList, the longer it takes to make a copy. When using these classes, you can optimize their performance by limiting the removal of elements from the beginning and the addition of elements for which there is no room.

Fortunately, the implementation of both of these classes uses the System.array-copy method to rearrange the underlying array. That array is rearranged when elements are added for which there is no room and when elements are removed (see PRAXIS 40). Using System.arraycopy makes this type of manipulation as efficient as possible.

Given the performance implications of the Vector and ArrayList, consider using an array in performance-critical code. If you require the functionality of a Vector but not its synchronization, use an ArrayList. Use the Vector only when you require both its functionality and its inherent synchronization.

Simply because you have a variable amount of data you want to store does not automatically mean you must use a Vector or an ArrayList. If you are not sure of the number of elements you need to store, you might consider creating an array big enough to hold your largest case. This could waste a lot of memory for your average case, but the performance advantages might outweigh the memory costs. Only through careful profiling and a detailed analysis of your system can you make the correct choice.

PRAXIS 42: **Reuse objects whenever possible**

Object creation is very expensive (see PRAXIS 32), therefore, you want to minimize the number of objects created. Fewer objects created means faster code. However, you might often need to create many objects or to create the same object repeatedly. PRAXES 32 and 43 outline techniques to help improve performance in many areas, including object creation. Another technique at your disposal is to reuse an existing object instead of creating a new one. Consider a class that represents an employee:

```
class Employee
{
  private String EmpName;
  private String EmpTitle;
  private int EmpNumber;

  public Employee()
  {}
  public Employee(String name, String title, int number)
  {
    EmpName = name;
    EmpTitle = title;
    EmpNumber = number;
  }

  public int salary()
  {
    int salary = 0;
    //Query database based on Employee object to get salary.
    salary = querydb(this);
    return salary;
  }

  public void setName(String name)
  {
    EmpName = name;
  }

  public void setTitle(String title)
  {
    EmpTitle = title;
  }
```

```
      public void setNumber(int number)
      {
        EmpNumber = number;
      }
  }
```

This class has methods to set its various fields and a method to return the salary of a given Employee object.

Now consider how this class might be used. For example, suppose that a method computes the total payroll of all employees. It receives as arguments three arrays of data. The first argument is an array of employee names, the second is an array of employee titles, and the third is an array of employee identification numbers. The method creates an object of the Employee class based on the data in the arrays, queries the salary of each employee, and calculates a total. The code might look like this:

```
    public int computePayroll(String[] name, String[] title,
                              int[] number)
    {
      int size = name.length;
      int totalPayroll = 0;
      for (int i=0; i<size; i++)
      {
        Employee emp = new Employee(name[i], title[i], number[i]);
        totalPayroll += emp.salary();
      }
      return totalPayroll;
    }
```

This code is inefficient. The problem is that a new object of the Employee class is unnecessarily created during each loop iteration. This is expensive and slows down the code. For this method, the Employee object can be created once and reused. A much more efficient implementation of this method is as follows:

```
    public int computePayroll(String[] name, String[] title,
                              int[] number)
    {
      int size = name.length;
      int totalPayroll = 0;
      if (size > 0)
      {
        Employee emp = new Employee();

        for (int i=0; i<size; i++)
        {
```

```
        emp.setName(name[i]);
        emp.setTitle(title[i]);
        emp.setNumber(number[i]);
        totalPayroll += emp.salary();
      }
    }
    return totalPayroll;
  }
```

This method creates only one instance of the Employee object and then reuses it as needed. It executes more than five times faster than the original implementation. For this technique to work, the class must provide methods to set the relevant fields for the object. For example, the Employee class provides setters for the name, title, and employee number fields. This allows you to create one object and set the relevant fields for each usage.

If a class does not provide these methods and you have access to the source code, you can use a more efficient technique. Instead of calling several methods to set the relevant fields of the object, provide a reinitialize method. This results in one method call instead of many. For example, the Employee class and the computePayroll method are modified to look like this:

```
class Employee
{
  //As before...
  public void reinitialize(String name, String title, int number)
  {
    EmpName = name;
    EmpTitle = title;
    EmpNumber = number;
  }
}

public int computePayroll(String[] name, String[] title,
                          int[] number)
{
  int size = name.length;
  int totalPayroll = 0;
  if (size > 0)
  {
    Employee emp = new Employee();
    for (int i=0; i<size; i++)
    {
      emp.reinitialize(name[i], title[i], number[i]);
      totalPayroll += emp.salary();
    }
  }
```

```
    return totalPayroll;
}
```

The `reinitialize` method is about 5 percent faster than the previous way to reinitialize the object. Although a modest gain, it can be significant if this technique is applied often.

Another consideration is whether reusing the object is valid. If the method you call stores the object reference, you cannot use this technique. For example, if you create objects of the `Employee` class and pass them to a method that stores them in a `Vector`, you cannot use this technique. The `Vector` class stores an object reference and does not make a copy of the object. To store a copy of the object, you need to clone it first. For additional information on cloning and code examples of cloning using `Vectors`, see PRAXES 64 and 66.

If the method makes a copy, or clone, of the object reference before storing it, you can reuse the object. In this case, you can effectively use this technique to produce more efficient code.

Reusing objects has an additional benefit: If an object is reused instead of unreferenced, the garbage collector has less work to do. The less work the garbage collector does, the less time it takes to run, and the faster your program runs.

PRAXIS 43: Use lazy evaluation

Lazy evaluation is a language-independent technique to delay computations until they are required. The delay of work is not what gives you better performance. Rather, the performance boost results when the delayed computations are never needed and, therefore, are not performed. Consequently, you avoid work that was never needed.

Consider an example of a large object that represents an employee. The object has many fields, some of which are other objects that contain various data about the employee. The creation of this object requires a unique identifier, which serves as a key into a database. The database contains all of the necessary information to build this object. Consider the following `Employee` class and its associated support classes:

```
class NameInfo
{
  private String lastName;
  private String firstName;
  private String middleName;
  private String courtesyTitle;
  //...
}

class ContactNumbers
{
  private String homeNumber;
  private String officeNumber;
  private String mobileNumber;
  private String faxNumber;
  //...
}

class EmergencyContactInfo
{
  private NameInfo name1;
  private ContactNumbers number1;
  private NameInfo name2;
  private ContactNumbers number2;
  //...
}

class AddressInfo
{
  private String street;
  private String city;
  private String state;
  private int    zip;
  //...
}

class WorkAddressInfo
{
  private AddressInfo workAddress;
  private String mailStop;
  //...
}

class Employee
{
  private NameInfo name;
  private String jobTitle;
  private String emailAddress;
  private ContactNumbers phoneNumbers;
  private EmergencyContactInfo emergencyContact;
```

```
    private AddressInfo homeAddress;
    private WorkAddressInfo workAddress;

    public Employee(int employeeID)
    {
      //Make multiple queries to a database to gather the
      //information about an Employee. Then build all of the parts
      //of the Employee object with the data.
      name = new NameInfo(...);
      jobTitle = new String(...);
      emailAddress = new String(...);
      phoneNumbers = new ContactNumbers(...);
      emergencyContact = new EmergencyContactInfo(...);
      homeAddress = new AddressInfo(...);
      workAddress = new WorkAddressInfo(...);
      //...
    }

    public AddressInfo homeAddr()
    {
      return homeAddress;
    }
    //...
  }
```

As you can see creating an object of the Employee class requires a read from a database and the creation of several aggregate objects. PRAXIS 32 discusses the high cost of object creation, especially for heavyweight objects. Objects of the Employee class are considered heavyweight because they contain many other objects. In addition, some of the objects in the Employee class contain other objects. This makes creating an object of the Employee class an expensive operation.

Assume code that creates objects of the Employee class does not necessarily use all of the data that is gathered during the construction of one of these objects. Consider code written like this:

```
    public void printHomeAddress(int employeeID)
    {
      Employee emp = new Employee(employeeID);
      AddressInfo addrinfo = emp.homeAddr();
      System.out.println("Street " + addrinfo.street());
      System.out.println("City " + addrinfo.city());
      System.out.println("State " + addrinfo.state());
      System.out.println("Zip " + addrinfo.zip());
    }
```

This code absorbs the entire expense of creating an Employee object, only to use one of its data members before the object goes out of scope at the end of the method. Remember, the constructor for Employee creates the entire object. This method uses only a small portion of the constructed data. The goal is to reduce the cost of object creation. One way to cut down on this expense is to make creating an object of the Employee class cheaper by utilizing *lazy evaluation.*

With lazy evaluation, you delay computations until they are required. Applying this technique to the Employee class means that you do not construct the entire object during the Employee class constructor. Instead, you simply initialize all of the fields to null. When methods on an Employee object are called, you construct the necessary portions of the object to satisfy the method call. For example, with these changes the Employee class and its constructor now look like this:

```
class Employee
{
  private NameInfo name;
  private String jobTitle;
  private String emailAddress;
  private ContactNumbers phoneNumbers;
  private EmergencyContactInfo emergencyContact;
  private AddressInfo homeAddress;
  private WorkAddressInfo workAddress;
  private int employeeID;

  public Employee(int eid)
  {
    employeeID = eid;
  }
  //...
}
```

When an object of the Employee class is created, the constructor's only function is to store the employeeID in the class instance data. This makes creating an Employee object very fast. All of the other instance data are set to null. The constructor does not have to set the other instance variables to null because null is their default value. When a class is initialized, all of its instance variables are set to their default values by the JVM before the body of the constructor is invoked. (For more details on this, see PRAXIS 37.)

After this change to the constructor, the methods of the Employee class also must change. For example, the homeAddr method of the Employee class changes to this:

```
public AddressInfo homeAddr()
{
  if (homeAddress == null)
  {
    //Query database based on stored employeeID and gather
    //information to create the AddressInfo object.
    homeAddress = new AddressInfo(...);
  }
  return homeAddress;
}
```

Now examine what happens when the `printHomeAddress` method is called. An `Employee` object is created but without any data. The constructor simply stores the `employeeID` field for later use. When the `homeAddr` method is called, this method checks whether the instance data `homeAddress` is `null`. If it is, the database is queried based on the stored `employeeID` field. The only data retrieved from the database is the data necessary to create an `AddressInfo` object, which is then returned. When the `printHomeAddress` method returns, the `Employee` object goes out of scope.

With lazy evaluation, you can save a great deal of time by not gathering data that is not used. Thus, creating the `Employee` object went from being very expensive to being very cheap.

This technique can also be used for numerical computations. Some computations are particularly expensive. Through judicious use of lazy evaluation, you can often speed up code significantly. For example, consider the following class for a matrix, which has methods to add and multiply two matrixes:

```
class Matrix2D
{
  private int[][] matrix;

  public Matrix2D(int sizex, int sizey)
  {
    matrix = new int[sizex][sizey];
    //...
  }
  public void addMatrix(Matrix2D other)
  {
    //Add other to this.
  }
  public void multiplyMatrix(Matrix2D other)
  {
    //Multiply other by this.
  }
```

```
      public int elementAt(int row, int col)
      {
        //Return element at row/col.
      }
      //...
    }
```

Code that utilizes this class might look like this:

```
    //...
    Matrix2D matrix1 = new Matrix2D(500,500);
    Matrix2D matrix2 = new Matrix2D(500,500);
    matrix1.multiplyMatrix(matrix2);
    matrix1.elementAt(275, 314);
    //...
```

This code creates two matrixes, multiplies them, and then retrieves one of the 250,000 elements. If the other 249,999 elements are not used before the modified matrix goes out of scope, virtually all of the work in multiplying the two matrixes is wasted. Even if three quarters of the elements in the matrix are accessed, then 62,500 matrix multiplication operations still remain, unused. This can represent a huge waste of processing time.

A better solution is to use lazy evaluation. When the addMatrix or multiply-Matrix method executes, instead of its performing the full matrix addition or multiplication, it simply does nothing, except store data about the action that just occurred on the matrix. Then, when specific areas of the matrix are accessed with the elementAt method, it calculates only what is needed and returns the data. In this way, it does only work that needs to be done and skips the work that does not. The following is an example of how to implement this technique:

```
    class Matrix2D
    {
      private int[][] matrix;
      private boolean performAdd;
      private boolean performMultiply;
      private Matrix2D mat;
      private boolean actionPending;
      private int width;
      private int height;

      public Matrix2D(int sizex, int sizey, int initialValue)
      {
        width = sizex;
        height = sizey;
```

```
      matrix = new int[sizex][sizey];  //Create the matrix and fill
      for (int i=0; i<sizex; i++)      //it with the default values.
        for (int j=0; j<sizey; j++)
          matrix[i][j] = initialValue;
    }

    public void addMatrix(Matrix2D other)
    {
      if (actionPending)  //Perform any pending actions first.
        performAction();
      performAdd = true;  //Store this action...
      performMultiply = false;
      mat = other;
      actionPending = true;
    }

    public void multiplyMatrix(Matrix2D other)
    {
      if (actionPending)   //Perform any pending actions first.
        performAction();
      performMultiply = true;  //Store this action...
      performAdd = false;
      mat = other;
      actionPending = true;
    }

    public int elementAt(int row, int col)
    {
      int value;
      if (performAdd)  //Perform the stored action, return result.
        value = (mat.matrix[row][col]) + (this.matrix[row][col]);
      else
        value = (mat.matrix[row][col]) * (this.matrix[row][col]);

      actionPending = false;
      return value;
    }

    private void performAction()
    {
      if (performAdd)  //Perform the pending action.
      {
        for (int i=0; i<width; i++)
          for (int j=0; j<height; j++)
            matrix[i][j] += mat.matrix[i][j];
      }
      else if (performMultiply)
      {
        for (int i=0; i<width; i++)
          for (int j=0; j<height; j++)
            matrix[i][j] *= mat.matrix[i][j];
```

```
            }
        }
        //...
    }
```

To save space, some of the error checking in the previous code is elided. Notice that this code keeps track of only one action at a time. For example, suppose that you create two objects of the `Matrix2D` class. The first object calls its `addMatrix` method, passing in the second matrix object. On this invocation, the `addMatrix` method simply stores the "add matrix" information about the action requested. If the `addMatrix` or `multiplyMatrix` methods are called before the `elementAt` method is called, the pending action is performed and the new action is stored. Additional code can be added to store further pending operations in order to potentially make the implementation more efficient.

Using this technique to minimize computations can have significant benefits for performance. Keep in mind, though, that lazy evaluation does not always result in faster code. In the previous matrix example, if all of the values of the matrix are accessed, the use of lazy evaluation is slower. This is because of the extra data and logic needed to support this technique. Lazy evaluation is useful only when you can avoid enough unnecessary computations to meet your performance goals. The strategy is to delay work that has a good chance of never needing to be done.

PRAXIS 44: Optimize source code by hand

PRAXIS 29 discusses that most Java compilers perform very few optimizations when compiling Java source code. Because the Java compiler does so little in the way of optimization, you can optimize your source code to make the compiler generate optimized bytecode. Typically, the better bytecode you provide a JVM, the faster your code will run.

This PRAXIS does not present an exhaustive list of all optimizations that can be performed on Java code. Optimizations can be very complicated and time consuming to implement. That is why they are typically best left to compilers. However, some of the easier and more common optimizations can be performed by hand without much extra effort and are included here.

Before implementing these optimizations, verify that the Java compiler you use does not perform them for you. Do this by examining the bytecode produced by

the Java compiler.[11] Use the javap tool with the -c option to disassemble the
.class file generated by javac. For example:

```
javac Test.java
javap -c Test > Test.bc
```

The javac invocation compiles the Test.java file and produces a .class file,
Test.class. The javap invocation disassembles the given .class file. The previous invocation saves the generated bytecode to the file Test.bc.

The following examples include several common optimization opportunities that
most Java compilers do not perform. Where appropriate, an example contains Java
source code that is a candidate for optimization, as well as the source rewritten to
include the optimization. The bytecode generated by the Java compiler for the
source is optionally shown for understanding and emphasis.

The following optimization techniques are examined:

- Empty method removal

- Dead code removal

- Strength reduction

- Constant folding

- Common subexpression elimination

- Loop unrolling

- Algebraic simplification

- Loop invariant code motion

Empty Method Removal

Methods that are now empty typically contained code at one time. Throughout the
development of a system, code in a method is removed by various programmers
until the method no longer performs the task it was originally implemented to perform. Consider the following code, which contains two empty methods that are
being called from main:

[11.] At the time of this writing, no Java compilers that I tried performed these simple
optimizations.

```
//Empty methods
class Test
{
  static void foo()
  {}
  final public void bar()
  {}
  public static void main(String args[])
  {
    Test t = new Test();
    t.foo();
    t.bar();
  }
}
```

The generated bytecode for methods main, foo, and bar is as follows:

```
Method void bar()
   0 return

Method void foo()
   0 return

Method void main(java.lang.String[])
   0 new #1 <Class Test>
   3 dup
   4 invokespecial #3 <Method Test()>
   7 astore_1
   8 invokestatic #6 <Method void foo()>
  11 aload_1
  12 invokevirtual #5 <Method void bar()>
  15 return
```

Even though methods foo and bar are empty and perform no functions, method main still calls them. These method calls can be safely eliminated, thereby making the code more efficient, as well as reducing the size of the generated .class file.

Empty methods should be flagged by the compiler. If your compiler does not do this, you can find empty methods at the end of the development cycle via a thorough examination of the code.

Dead Code Removal

PRAXIS 29 shows two cases in which the Java compiler removes unreachable, or dead, code. Dead code, however, can occur more obscurely and the Java compiler does not eliminate it. It can be caused by sloppy programming, or by numerous modifications to the same code. As logic is changed, code can become unreach-able. This extra code unnecessarily increases the `.class` file size. Removing dead code can also produce more simplistic and more easily understood logic. For example, consider the following:

```
int j = 5;
int[] a = new int[10];
for (int i=0; i<10; i++)
{
  a[i] = j;
  if (j == 5)
    a[i] = 25;
  else
    a[i] = 10;
}
```

The logic in this loop results in code that never executes. The loop always assigns 25 to a[i]. The code should be rewritten like this:

```
int[] a = new int[10];
for (int i=0; i<10; i++)
  a[i] = 25;
```

The rewritten loop is about 4 percent faster than the original. It also is much clearer and intuitive. After the loop is written in this way, further optimizations can then be performed. See Loop Unrolling on page 157.

Strength Reduction

Strength reduction involves replacing an expensive operation with a more efficient one. A common optimization is to use the compound assignment operators. For example, consider the following code and expression:

```
int x = 5;
int[] a = new int[N];
for (int i=0; i<N; i++)
  a[i] = a[i] + x;
```

The generated bytecode for the line a[i] + a[i] + x is:

```
11 aload_2
12 iload_3
13 aload_2
14 iload_3
15 iaload
```

```
16 iload_1
17 iadd
18 iastore
```

Now consider the loop rewritten with a compound assignment operator:

```
int x = 5;
int[] a = new int[N];
for (int i=0; i<N; i++)
  a[i] += x;
```

The bytecode generated for the line a[i] += x is:

```
11 aload_2
12 iload_3
13 dup2
14 iaload
15 iload_1
16 iadd
17 iastore
```

The two sets of generated bytecode differ in one way. The bytecode for the compound assignment uses the dup2 opcode at location 13 to duplicate the top two words on the stack. The top two words are the array a and the loop index i. The first example pushes these values onto the stack with the aload_2 and iload 3 instructions. Duplicating the top two words on the stack is faster with the dup2 instruction than with two separate instructions. The rewritten code with the compound assignment operator is about 10 percent faster than the original code.

This technique can produce significant performance savings if performed repeatedly in a loop. In addition, because less code is generated, a space savings is realized because the .class file is smaller.

Constant Folding

PRAXIS 29 demonstrates that the compiler performs simple constant folding. Data, however, must be declared final in order for the compiler to optimize it. For example, the following code:

```
static int a = 30;
static int b = 60;
int c = a + b + 100;
```

is compiled into the following bytecode:

```
0 getstatic #6 <Field int a>    //Push the value for a.
3 getstatic #7 <Field int b>    //Push the value for b.
6 iadd                          //Pop a and b, push their sum.
7 bipush 100                    //Push 100.
9 iadd                          //Pop sum and 100, push their sum.
10 istore_1                     //Pop sum and store it at index 1
                                //of the local variable table(c).
```

The expression for variable c is not optimized by the compiler. Because variables a and b are not declared final and therefore are not constant, the addition is performed at runtime. Declaring the variables a and b as final allows them to be treated as constants by the compiler so it can perform the optimization. Thus, the modified code:

```
static final int a = 30;
static final int b = 60;
int c = a + b + 100;
```

is compiled into the following bytecode:

```
0 sipush 190      //Push 190.
3 istore_1        //Pop 190 and store at index 1 of the local
                  //variable table(c).
```

Because the variables are declared final, the addition takes place at compile time and the bytecode works with a constant value. Therefore, when declaring data that has a constant value, use the final keyword in order to allow the compiler to optimize the expression.

Common Subexpression Elimination

Common expressions are sometimes coded repeatedly for code clarity. You should eliminate duplicate expressions and provide a temporary variable instead. For example:

```
SomeObject[] someObj = new SomeObject[N];
someObj[i+j] = new SomeObject();
someObj[i+j].foo(k);
someObj[i+j].foo(k+1);
someObj[i+j].foo(k+2);
someObj[i+j].foo(k+3);
someObj[i+j].foo(k+4);
```

The common subexpression, someObj[i+j], can be eliminated and replaced with a more efficient construct. For example:

```
SomeObject[] someObj = new SomeObject[N];
someObj[i+j] = new SomeObject();
SomeObject tempObj = someObj[i+j];   //Create temporary
tempObj.foo(k);                      //Use it...
tempObj.foo(k+1);
tempObj.foo(k+2);
tempObj.foo(k+3);
tempObj.foo(k+4);
```

For many iterations, the optimized code is twice as fast as the original code, and it is smaller.

Loop Unrolling

Unrolling a loop has the advantage of eliminating the code for the loop construct and branching, thereby resulting in faster execution. Its disadvantage is that more code is generated, thereby resulting in a larger .class file. A typical loop might be coded like this:

```
int[] ia = new int[4];
for (int i=0; i<4; i++)
   ia[i] = 10;
```

and unrolled like this:

```
int[] ia = new int[4];
ia[0] = 10;
ia[1] = 10;
ia[2] = 10;
ia[3] = 10;
```

This particular unrolled loop is about 7 percent faster than the original version.

Algebraic Simplification

Algebraic simplification involves using the rules of algebra to simplify expressions. This simplification can lead to smaller and faster code. For example, consider the following code:

```
int a = 1; int b = 2; int c = 3;
int d = 4; int e = 5; int f = 6;
int x = (f*a)+(f*b)+(f*c)+(f*d)+(f*e);
```

This code involves four additions and five multiplications. Using the rules of algebra, you can rewrite and simplify this code as follows:

```
int a = 1; int b = 2; int c = 3;
int d = 4; int e = 5; int f = 6;
int x = f*(a+b+c+d+e);
```

This rewritten code still has four additions, but it has eliminated all but one of the multiplications. This expression is simpler and generates smaller and faster code than the original.

Loop Invariant Code Motion

A loop invariant consists of an expression that exists in a loop but which can be safely moved outside of the loop body. This saves the time required to calculate the expression for each loop iteration. (An example of this is used in PRAXIS 29 and is repeated here for clarity.) Consider the following code:

```
int a = 10;
int b = 20;
int[] arr = new int[val];
for (int i=0; i<val; i++)
  arr[i] = a + b;
```

The loop invariant is the code that adds a and b. This addition can safely be moved outside of the loop, thus making the loop more efficient. This code is rewritten as follows:

```
int a = 10;
int b = 20;
int c = a + b;
int[] arr = new int[val];
for (int i=0; i<val; i++)
  arr[i] = c;
```

Removing loop invariants can have dramatic performance benefits for programs because a large amount of execution time typically is spent in loops.

Although the examples in this PRAXIS are simple to understand and follow, finding opportunities for these optimizations in real code is often more difficult. Programmers who are aware of optimization techniques learn to spot them quickly as they write and review code. These types of hand tuning will not be necessary if Java compilers and JITs improve over time. It is still useful, however, to know about and use these techniques until the availability of better optimization tools.

PRAXIS 45: Compile to native code

In a quest for fast code, some programmers believe they must trade the platform portability of Java for raw speed. This is done by compiling Java source code to native binary code for the particular target on which the code runs. Instead of the Java source being compiled to the intermediate bytecode form, it is compiled directly to native machine instructions.

The advantage of doing this is that you no longer have the overhead involved in converting the intermediate bytecode form to native binary code at runtime. This typically results in faster-executing code. Its disadvantage is the platform portability of Java is usually lost, although that might not be a problem. There is at least one solution to this problem that does not require the loss of platform portability, yet it derives the benefits of native binary code execution.

First, consider complete static code generation, whereby you plan to give up Java's platform portability. If the code is required to run only on one machine, then static code generation might be a partial solution to performance problems. An example of using this technique is when writing code for a server application. The code is going to run on one server, and it must be very fast.

Static code generation is also useful when writing code for an embedded device. The device might have very small memory requirements. Compiling Java to native binary code might solve this problem because you will benefit from the reduced size of the runtime needed for the code.

Various vendors have native solutions for Java. Many of these solutions have one thing in common: They treat Java as simply a programming language and not as the cross-platform and portable solution it was designed to be. You should consider the completeness of the vendor's solution. For example, does its solution support dynamic class loading? Are there other features of Java that you rely on that the solution does not offer?

Programmers often think that if they decide to statically compile Java, they eliminate the need for the JVM. This is not entirely true, depending on which native solution is used. Statically compiling to native binary code presents a problem with garbage collection. If all code is compiled to native binary code, how is garbage collection going to work without a JVM?

Various vendors have different solutions to this problem. One is to statically compile Java but still deploy it on the target system with a small virtual machine that performs garbage collection. This solution is advantageous because you do not have to consider memory management. You do not, however, have as small a program as you might need.

A second solution elected by some vendors is to add a `delete` keyword to their Java-like language. The disadvantage is that adding something that is not part of *The Java*™ *Language Specification*[12] immediately makes any code you write non-portable to compliant Java implementations. The advantage of this approach is you eliminate the need for a runtime to perform garbage collection. And the disadvantage of *that* is that the garbage collection is performed by the programmer who writes the code, by using the special `delete` keyword.

Another solution is to consider compiling portions of your program to native binary code while maintaining Java's platform portability. This allows you to retain Java's benefits, such as garbage collection and dynamic class loading, while having selected, performance-critical methods compiled into native binary code. This is accomplished with tools that compile particular Java methods into optimized native code that is then accessed though the JNI (Java Native Interface). This solution offers the best of both worlds. You maintain Java's platform portability, while taking advantage of the performance benefits of executing optimized native methods.

Carefully consider the advantages and disadvantages of compiling to native binary code. After you weigh what you gain and what you lose, you are then able to make an informed decision about the trade-offs.

---

12. *The Java*™ *Language Specification*, James Gosling, Bill Joy, Guy Steele, Addison-Wesley, 1996.

Multithreading

*For ease and speed in doing a thing do not give
the work lasting solidity or exactness of beauty.*
—Plutarch, *Life of Pericles*

WRITING multithreaded code properly is one of the most complex tasks in programming. The concepts are fairly straightforward, but writing a correct implementation of code that utilizes multiple threads of execution is a daunting task.

Writing multithreaded code in Java is easier than writing it in other languages. This is both a blessing and a curse. For programmers who are skilled in multithreaded programming techniques, Java language support for multithreading is a welcome addition. The curse is that the language support leads some to believe that writing multithreaded code is somehow easy.

More bugs are introduced into programs through the implementation of concurrency than most other technologies. While writing properly behaved multithreaded code is complex, debugging it is even more complex.

Before writing multithreaded code, programmers must have a solid grasp of concurrent programming principles. Otherwise, they have no chance of writing multithreaded code that behaves correctly.

This section covers some intermediate to advanced multithreading topics. It answers some questions about Java's multithreading support. For example, what does the synchronized keyword really do to code? What is the difference between synchronized instance methods and synchronized static methods? Is atomic assignment really thread safe? How do you safely stop a thread? The section also offers advice and examples concerning the use of the various constructs and issues that programmers commonly face when writing multithreaded code.

PRAXIS 46: Understand that for instance methods, synchronized locks objects, not methods or code

The synchronized keyword is used as either a method modifier or as a statement inside of a method. This dual usage causes some confusion about exactly what the synchronized keyword does. It is often described in terms of mutual exclusion (mutex) or a critical section. This causes many programmers to incorrectly think that because code is protected by synchronized, it can be accessed by only one thread at a time.

For instance methods, the synchronized keyword does not lock a method or code; it locks objects. (See PRAXIS 47 for a discussion of synchronized used with statics.) Remember that there is only one lock associated with each object.

When synchronized is used as a method modifier, the lock obtained is that for the object on which the method was invoked. When it is used on an object reference, the lock obtained is that for the object referred to. For example, consider the following code:

```
class Test
{
  public synchronized void method1()
  {
    //...
  }

  public void method2()
  {
    synchronized(this) {
      //...
    }
  }

  public void method3(SomeObject someObj)
  {
    //...
    synchronized(someObj) {
      //...
    }
  }
}
```

The first two methods, method1 and method2, are functionally identical regarding the object being locked. (They differ in the amount of code generated and in how they perform. For details on this, see PRAXIS 34.) Both methods are synchronized on this. In other words, a lock is obtained for the object on which the method was invoked. Because both methods are of the class Test, the lock is obtained for an object of class Test. The method3 method is synchronized on the object referenced by someObj.

What exactly does it mean to synchronize on an object? It means that the thread that invoked the method has that object's lock. To hold an object's lock means another thread requesting a lock for the same object through a synchronized method or a synchronized statement cannot obtain that lock until it is released. However, another thread executing the same synchronized method or block on a *different* instance of the same class *can* obtain that instance's lock.

Thus, code in a synchronized method or block can be executed at the same time by multiple threads if the method is invoked on two different objects. For example, consider the following code:

```java
class Foo extends Thread
{
  private int val;
  public Foo(int v)
  {
    val = v;
  }

  public synchronized void printVal(int v)
  {
    while(true)
      System.out.println(v);
  }

  public void run()
  {
    printVal(val);
  }
}

class Bar extends Thread
{
  private Foo sameFoo;
  public Bar(Foo f)
  {
    sameFoo = f;
  }
```

```
    public void run()
    {
      sameFoo.printVal(2);
    }
}

class Test
{
  public static void main(String args[])
  {
    Foo f1 = new Foo(1);
    f1.start();
    Bar b = new Bar(f1);
    b.start();
    Foo f2 = new Foo(3);
    f2.start();
  }
}
```

Class Foo contains a synchronized method, printVal. This method is executed by three different threads. You might think that because printVal is declared synchronized, it is executed by only one thread at a time. However, this code demonstrates that even though the printVal method is declared synchronized, it can be executed by multiple threads concurrently. Running this code generates output of the form:

```
1
1
1
1
3
3
3
3
1
1
1
3
3
3
```

What might be surprising is the interleaved execution of two of the threads. If only one thread could execute a synchronized method at a time, you would never see interleaved output. In fact, what happens is the code that prints the 1's and 3's is executing the printVal method concurrently. Examining this code shows why this happens.

An object of the class `Foo`, referenced by `f1`, is created, passing the value 1, and then run on another thread. The `run` method of class `Foo` is called, which then calls the `synchronized printVal` method. When the `printVal` method is entered, it has obtained the lock for the `Foo` object. It then begins printing the value 1. Because it has entered an infinite loop, the lock for this `Foo` object is never released.

Then an object of type `Bar`, referenced by `b`, is created, passing the same `Foo` object currently in use. It is run on another thread and calls the same `printVal` method, with the value 2, on the same `Foo` object. Because the `printVal` method is `synchronized`, this call attempts to obtain the lock for the object on which the method is called. The `printVal` method is called on the same `Foo` object as the previous invocation, so this call blocks until the first execution of the `printVal` method is finished. Because the first thread holds this lock and is in an infinite loop, the code never outputs both a 1 and a 2. The first thread to obtain the lock blocks out the other thread forever. Therefore, you do not see any interleaved execution of these two invocations of the `printVal` method.

Finally, a second object of the `Foo` class, referenced by `f2`, is created, passing the value 3, and then run on a third thread. The `run` method of class `Foo` is called, which then calls the `synchronized printVal` method. When that method is called, it attempts to obtain the lock for the object on which it is called. The attempt to get this lock succeeds regardless of whether the thread for `f1` or `b` still holds a lock. Because this invocation of the `printVal` method is called on a *different* object, it can obtain that object's lock.

Thus, you can see interleaved execution between the threads for `f1` and `f2`, but never between the threads for `b` and `f1`. The threads for `f1` and `f2` operate on unique objects and therefore are not affected by the `synchronized` keyword. The threads for `f1` and `b`, however, operate on the same `Foo` object and therefore must synchronize on its lock.

Remember that synchronization locks objects, not methods or code. Simply because a method, or section of code, is declared `synchronized` does not necessarily mean it is executed by only one thread at a time. This is important if the code in the `synchronized` method or block alters a mutually shared resource.

If the code alters an instance variable of the object, no problem results. In the previous example, `f1` and `f2` are two distinct objects and therefore contain two distinct instance variables. If the `printVal` method alters the instance variable `val`, then the code works as expected without conflict because the threads for `f1` and f2 alter different data. However, if the printVal method shares some other non-object resource, such as a static variable, a conflict might result. In this case, you must synchronize on a mutually shared object in order to prevent conflicts. (PRAXES 47 and 49 provide examples of this technique.)

One final note about the synchronized keyword. The Java language does not allow constructors to be declared synchronized. (A compiler error is generated if the synchronized keyword is present on a constructor declaration.) This is because two threads that call the same constructor concurrently operate on two distinct pieces of memory for two distinct instances of the same class. However, if these constructors contain code that contends for a mutually shared resource, you must synchronize on that resource in order to avoid conflicts.

PRAXIS 47: Distinguish between synchronized statics and synchronized instance methods

The synchronized keyword can be applied to static methods and class literals as well as instance methods and objects. The lock obtained when using the synchronized keyword for statics differs than that for non-statics. When a synchronized static method is invoked, the lock obtained is the lock associated with the Class object for the class in which the method is defined. When a synchronized block is invoked on a class literal, the lock obtained is the same, that is, the lock associated with the specified Class object. Consider the following class:

```
class Tournament
{
  public synchronized static void foo()
  {
    //...
  }
  public void bar()
  {
    synchronized(Tournament.class) {
    //...
    }
  }
}
```

Both method foo and method bar obtain the same lock. The lock obtained is the lock for the Tournament class object. foo acquires the lock with the synchronized method modifier, whereas bar acquires the lock using the class literal Tournament.class.

When synchronized is applied to instance methods and object references, the lock obtained is different. For instance methods, the lock is that for the object on which the method was invoked. Synchronizing on an object obtains the lock for the specified object (see PRAXIS 46).

Because of the different locks obtained when synchronizing on instance methods and objects, or static methods and class literals, care must be taken when determining mutual exclusion behavior. For example, consider the following code:

```
class Foo implements Runnable
{
  public synchronized void printM1()
  {
    while (true)
      System.out.println("printM1");
  }

  public synchronized static void printM2()
  {
    while (true)
      System.out.println("printM2");
  }
  public void run()
  {
    printM1();
  }
}

class Test
{
  public static void main(String args[])
  {
    Foo f = new Foo();
    Thread t = new Thread(f);
    t.start();
    f.printM2();
  }
}
```

This code creates an object of the class Foo and a secondary thread on which to execute its code. The secondary thread simply calls the synchronized printM1 instance method, which then prints the string printM1 in an infinite loop. The primary thread then calls the synchronized static method printM2. This method enters its own infinite loop to print the string printM2.

Because these methods are invoked on separate threads, they attempt to execute concurrently. You might think that because both methods are declared synchronized, the execution of the two threads cannot interleave between the two methods. You might also think that the output of this code is either the string printM1 or printM2, depending on which thread enters its synchronized method first and obtains the lock. After all, both methods are declared with the synchronized keyword.

Despite both methods' being declared synchronized, they are not thread safe. This is because one is a synchronized static method and the other is a synchronized instance method. Thus, they obtain two different locks. The instance method printM1 obtains the lock for the Foo object. The static method printM2 obtains the lock for the Class object of class Foo. These two locks are different and do not affect one another. When this code is executed, both strings are printed to the screen. In other words, execution interleaves between the two methods.

What if this code needs to be synchronized? For example, both methods might share a common resource. To protect the resource, the code must be properly synchronized in order to avoid a conflict. There are two options to solve this problem:

1. Synchronize on the common resource.

2. Synchronize on a special instance variable.

Option 1 involves simply adding synchronized statements in the methods in order to synchronize on the shared resource. For example, if these two methods were updating a global object, they would synchronize on it. The code might look like this:

```
class Foo implements Runnable
{
  private SomeObj someobj;
  public void printM1()
  {
    synchronized(someobj) {
      //The code to protect.
    }
  }

  public static void printM2(Foo f)
  {
    synchronized(f.someobj) {
      //The code to protect.
```

```
      }
    }
    //...
}
```

The second option involves declaring a local instance variable for the sole purpose
of synchronizing on it. This is implemented as follows:

```
class Foo implements Runnable
{
  private byte[] lock = new byte[0];
  public void printM1()
  {
    synchronized(lock) {
      //The code to protect.
    }
  }

  public static void printM2(Foo f)
  {
    synchronized(f.lock) {
      //The code to protect.
    }
  }
  //...
}
```

Because you can only lock objects, the local instance variable you use must be an
object. A zero element array is used because such an array is cheaper to create
than any other object. For example:

```
byte[] lock = new byte[0];
```

generates the following bytecode:

```
0 iconst_0          //Push 0.
1 newarray byte     //Pop 0 and create a new byte array with
                    //size 0. Push the newly created array
                    //reference(lock).
3 astore_1          //Pop the array reference(lock) and store it
                    //at index 1 of the local variable table.
```

Compare this to:

```
Object lock = new Object();
```

which generates this bytecode:

```
0 new #2 <Class java.lang.Object>
                        //Create an object of type java.lang.Object
                        //and push a reference to it(lock).
3 dup                   //Duplicate the top stack value and push it.
4 invokespecial #3 <Method java.lang.Object()>
                        //Pop the object reference(lock), and invoke
                        //its constructor.
7 astore_1              //Pop the object reference(lock) and store
                        //it at index 1 of the local variable table.
```

Creating a zero element array does not require a constructor call like the creation of `Object` does. It therefore executes faster. In addition, a `byte` array is used because it is often represented more compactly than an `int` array.

Either option results in code that is thread safe. Remember that synchronizing on an instance method or object reference obtains a completely different lock than code that synchronizes on a static method or class literal. Simply because two methods are declared `synchronized` does not necessarily mean they are thread safe. You must be careful to recognize and distinguish between the different locks obtained with synchronization.

PRAXIS 48: Use `private` data with an accessor method instead of `public` or `protected` data

The purpose of writing code with `synchronized` methods is to protect data from corruption. To properly protect data, you must ensure that it is declared and accessed correctly. Failure to correctly protect data allows users of your class to bypass whatever synchronization mechanisms you have in place.

For example, consider the following class that contains two methods that operate on an array. The array is declared as instance data of the class. Both methods are declared `synchronized` to ensure that data is not added and subtracted from the array concurrently. Is this class thread safe?

```
class Test implements Runnable
{
  public int[] intArray = new int[10];

  public synchronized void addToArray(int[] ar)
  {
    int len = intArray.length;
    if (len == ar.length)
    {
```

```
      for (int i=0; i<len; i++)  //Add array ar to intArray
      {
        System.out.println(intArray[i]);
        intArray[i] += ar[i];
      }
    }
  }

  public synchronized void subtractFromArray(int[] ar)
  {
    int len = intArray.length;
    if (len == ar.length)
    {
      for (int i=0; i<len; i++)  //Subtract array ar from intArray
        intArray[i] -= ar[i];
    }
  }

  public void run()
  {
    int[] a = new int[10];
    addToArray(a);
  }
  //...
}
```

This class is not thread safe. Even though the methods that share the array are declared synchronized, a problem remains. Because the data is not declared private, another thread can bypass the synchronized methods and access the data directly. For example:

```
Test tst = new Test();
Thread t = new Thread(tst);
t.start();
tst.intArray = null;
```

This code creates an object of the class Test and executes the code of the object on a secondary thread. The primary thread then directly accesses the public data of the class Test and sets the intArray field to null. When the secondary thread makes a call to the synchronized addToArray method, this method throws a NullPointerException. This occurs because the main thread set the intArray variable to null while the addToArray method was executing.

This problem exists because the intArray member is not private. If it were, there would be no way for the main thread to directly access it. Any data that is to be fully protected in a synchronized method must also be private to the class.

This is the only way to ensure that the data is protected against corruption and the class is thread safe. The correct implementation of this class is as follows:

```
class Test implements Runnable
{
  private int[] intArray = new int[10];

  //As before...
}
```

This class is now thread safe. However, what happens if you add a `public` accessor method that returns an object reference to the `intArray` field that is now `private`? For example, is this class still thread safe?

```
class Test implements Runnable
{
  private int[] intArray = new int[10];

  public int[] integerArray()
  {
    return intArray;
  }
  //As before...
}
```

This class is not thread safe. The problem is the `integerArray` method returns an object reference to the `private` data member `intArray`. This means that code could be written as follows:

```
Test tst = new Test();
Thread t = new Thread(tst);
t.start();
int[] temp = tst.integerArray();
temp[5] = 1;
```

Because the `integerArray` method returns an object reference to the `intArray` field, this code can now change the contents of the array while the `addToArray` method is executing. You can fix this problem by providing a `synchronized` method that clones the `intArray` field and returns a reference to a newly created cloned array object. This results in the `integerArray` method's returning a reference to a different array object than is referred to by the `intArray` field. For example:

```
class Test implements Runnable
{
  private int[] intArray = new int[10];

  public synchronized int[] integerArray()
  {
    return (int[])intArray.clone();
  }
  //As before...
}
```

This class is now thread safe. The `integerArray` method must be declared `synchronized` to ensure that the array is not changed during the cloning process. The addition of the clone is more expensive but is required for thread safety. For a detailed analysis of cloning, including shallow and deep cloning, see PRAXES 64 and 66.

Remember, for data that can be modified in a `synchronized` method, make the data `private` and optionally provide an accessor method. If the accessor method returns a reference to a mutable object, the object must be cloned first.

PRAXIS 49: Avoid unnecessary synchronization

Java provides synchronization to allow multiple threads of execution to access the same objects safely. Adding unneeded synchronization is nearly as bad as omitting necessary synchronization. Sometimes, programmers in search of thread-safe code synchronize too many methods. Excess synchronization can lead to code that deadlocks or code that runs slow. (For more on the cost of synchronization, see PRAXIS 34.) One main goal of your software is to run efficiently and without deadlocks. You should avoid unnecessary synchronization.

Because of the way the `synchronized` keyword is implemented, the result is often unnecessary synchronization and less concurrency. For example, consider the following class:

```
class Test
{
  private int[] ia1;
  private int[] ia2;
  private double[] da1;
  private double[] da2;
```

```
public synchronized void method1()
{
  //Access ia1 and ia2
}
public synchronized void method2()
{
  //Access ia1 and ia2
}
public synchronized void method3()
{
  //Access da1 and da2
}
public synchronized void method4()
{
  //Access da1 and da2
}
//...
}
```

This class is certainly thread safe. Each method must be declared synchronized in order to ensure the arrays are not corrupted by multiple threads accessing this object concurrently. For example, because method1 and method2 both access and potentially alter the arrays ia1 and ia2, access to them must be synchronized. The same is true of method3 and method4.

Notice, however, that although method1 and method2 must be synchronized with each other, they do not need to be synchronized with either method3 or method4. This is because method1 and method2 do not operate on data that method3 and method4 operate on. This is similarly true for method3 and method4 with regard to method1 and method2.

Unfortunately, this is how instance methods are sometimes synchronized in classes. However, synchronization in Java is not very granular. Synchronization provides you with only one lock per object. In the previous code, if you create an object of class Test and call method1 on the main thread and method3 on a secondary thread, you pay an unnecessary performance penalty. These methods synchronize with one another even though there is no need for them to do so. Remember that when a method is declared synchronized, the lock obtained is the lock for the object on which the method is invoked. Therefore, both methods attempt to get the same lock.

To fix the problem in the previous code you need multiple locks per object. Because Java does not provide this, you must furnish your own mechanism. One way to accomplish this is to create objects as instance data that serve only to provide locks. (For a discussion of why this code uses a zero element `byte` array for the lock object, see PRAXIS 47.) The previous code is modified using this technique and looks like this:

```java
class Test
{
  private int[] ia1;
  private int[] ia2;
  private double[] da1;
  private double[] da2;
  private byte[] lock1 = new byte[0];
  private byte[] lock2 = new byte[0];

  public void method1()
  {
    synchronized(lock1) {
      //Access ia1 and ia2
    }
  }
  public void method2()
  {
    synchronized(lock1) {
      //Access ia1 and ia2
    }
  }
  public void method3()
  {
    synchronized(lock2) {
      //Access da1 and da2
    }
  }
  public void method4()
  {
    synchronized(lock2) {
      //Access da1 and da2
    }
  }
  //...
}
```

Notice that this code no longer has `synchronized` methods. They are removed and replaced with `synchronized` blocks. This allows the synchronization to occur on different objects and allows the methods that can safely run concurrently to do so. For example, `method1` is able to execute concurrently with `method3` or `method4` because they access different object locks.

Care must be taken when using this technique. You must be sure that the methods you think can operate without synchronization are able to do so without causing errors. Debugging multithreaded code can be very time consuming, so it is important not to use this technique casually.

You might wonder why method1 and method2 do not lock both ia1 and ia2 instead of the lock1 object. This could be done, but it is more error prone. When you lock multiple objects, you must make sure to lock them in the same order throughout your code. Failure to do this can result in deadlock. For more on this problem and how to avoid it, see PRAXIS 52.

PRAXIS 50: Use synchronized or volatile when accessing shared variables

When variables are shared between threads, they must always be accessed properly in order to ensure that correct and valid values are manipulated. The JVM is guaranteed to treat reads and writes of data of 32 bits or less as atomic. This might lead some programmers to believe that access to shared variables does not need to be synchronized or the variables declared volatile. Consider this code:

```
class RealTimeClock
{
  private int clkID;
  private long clockTime;

  public int clockID()
  {
    return clkID;
  }
  public void setClockID(int id)
  {
    clkID = id;
  }

  public long time()
  {
    return clockTime;
  }
  public void setTime(long t)
  {
    clockTime = t;
  }
  //...
}
```

Now contemplate an implementation that uses the previous code. It might create an object of the `RealTimeClock` class and two threads. It then could call the methods of this class from the two threads.

The variables `clkID` and `clockTime` are stored in main memory. However, the Java language allows threads to keep *private working* copies of these variables. This enables a more efficient execution of the two threads. For example, when each thread reads and writes these variables, they can do so on the private working copies instead of accessing the variables from main memory. The private working copies are reconciled with main memory only at specific synchronization points.

The `clockID` and `setClockID` methods perform only a read and a write, respectively, on data of type `int`. Therefore, the operation of these methods is automatically atomic. However, given that the `clkID` variable could be stored in private working memory for each thread, consider the following possible sequence of events:

1. Thread 1 calls the `setClockID` method, passing a value of 5.

2. Thread 2 calls the `setClockID` method, passing a value of 10.

3. Thread 1 calls the `clockID` method, which returns the value 5.

This sequence of events is possible because the `clkID` variable is not guaranteed to be reconciled with main memory. During step 1, thread 1 places the value 5 in its working memory. When step 2 executes, thread 2 places the value 10 in its working memory. When step 3 executes, thread 1 reads the value from its working memory and returns 5. At no point are the values reconciled with main memory.

There are two ways to fix this problem.

1. Access the `clkID` variable from a `synchronized` method or block.

2. Declare the `clkID` variable `volatile`.

Either solution requires the `clkID` variable to be reconciled with main memory. Accessing the `clkID` variable from a `synchronized` method or block does not allow that code to execute concurrently, but it does guarantee that the `clkID` variable in main memory is updated appropriately. Main memory is updated when the object lock is obtained before the protected code executes, and then when the lock is released after the protected code executes.

177

Declaring the clkID variable volatile allows the code to execute concurrently and also guarantees that the private working copy of the clkID variable is reconciled with main memory. This reconciliation, however, occurs each time the variable is accessed.

Also consider the time and setTime methods that operate on a variable of type long. These methods can exhibit the same problem described previously. They also have an additional problem. Data of type long is typically represented by 64 bits spread across two 32-bit words. An implementation of the JVM might treat the operation on a 64-bit value as atomic, but most JVM implementations today do not, instead treating such operations as two distinct 32-bit operations.[1] Consider the following possible sequence of events with the clockTime instance variable:

1. Thread 1 calls the time method.

2. Thread 1 begins to read the clockTime instance variable and reads the first 32 bits.

3. Thread 1 is preempted by thread 2.

4. Thread 2 calls the setTime method. The setTime method performs two writes of 32 bits each to the clockTime instance variable, replacing both 32-bit values with different values.

5. Thread 2 is preempted by thread 1.

6. Thread 1 reads the second 32 bits of the clockTime instance variable and returns the result.

According to this sequence of events, the value returned by the time method is made up of the first 32 bits of the old value of the clockTime instance variable, and the second 32 bits of the new value of the same instance variable. The value returned is not correct. This is because of the multiple reads and writes necessary for 64-bit data in the JVM. The private working memory and main memory issue discussed earlier is also a problem. You have the same two options to fix this problem: Synchronize access to the clockTime variable, or declare it volatile.

---

[1] Implementations of JVMs are encouraged to treat 64-bit operations as atomic but are not required to do so. This is because some popular microprocessors currently do not provide efficient atomic memory transactions on 64-bit values.

In summary, it is important to understand that atomic operations do not automatically mean thread-safe operations. In addition, whenever multiple threads share variables it is important that they are accessed in a synchronized method or block, or arc declared with the volatile keyword. This ensures that the variables are properly reconciled with main memory, thereby guaranteeing correct values at all times.

Whether you use volatile or synchronized depends on several factors. If concurrency is important and you are not updating many variables, consider using volatile. If you are updating many variables, however, using volatile might be slower than using synchronization. Remember that when variables are declared volatile, they are reconciled with main memory on every access. By contrast, when synchronized is used, the variables are reconciled with main memory only when the lock is obtained and when the lock is released.

Consider using synchronized if you are updating many variables and do not want the cost of reconciling each of them with main memory on every access, or you want to eliminate concurrency for another reason.

The following table summarizes the differences between the synchronized and volatile keywords.

Table 4: volatile and synchronized

Technique	Advantages	Disadvantages
synchronized	Private working memory is reconciled with main memory when the lock is obtained and when the lock is released.	Eliminates concurrency.
volatile	Allows concurrency.	Private working memory is reconciled with main memory on each variable access.

PRAXIS 51:   Lock all objects involved in a single operation

Often, a method operates on more than one object. Simply synchronizing the method does not necessarily make the code thread safe. You must carefully analyze what objects are manipulated and how.

If a `synchronized` method calls a non-`synchronized` instance method to modify an object, it is thread safe. This is because a non-`synchronized` method becomes `synchronized` when called from a `synchronized` method. By contrast, if a `synchronized` method directly modifies objects that are not part of the `private` instance data of a method's class, the code is not thread safe.

For example, consider the following code that calculates the sum of two arrays. Assume that the array objects passed to this method are not part of the instance data of the object.

```
public synchronized int sumArrays(int[] a1, int[] a2)
{
  int value = 0;
  int size = a1.length;
  if (size == a2.length)
  {
    for (int i=0; i<size; i++)
      value += a1[i] + a2[i];
  }
  return value;
}
```

The problem with this code is that even though the method is declared `synchronized`, the objects it operates on are not. The `synchronized` keyword locks objects, not methods or code (see PRAXIS 46). The `sumArrays` method, therefore, can be executing on one thread while another thread changes the values of the unlocked array objects. This situation produces incorrect results.

It is sometimes not enough simply to synchronize a method. In such situations, you must specifically synchronize the objects that are accessed in the method. For this code to work properly, you must lock the array objects before accessing them to ensure they are not changed during the summation loop. Thus, the previous code is modified to look like this:

```
public int sumArrays(int[] a1, int[] a2)
{
  int value = 0;
  int size = a1.length;
```

```
      if (size == a2.length)
      {
        synchronized(a1) {
          synchronized(a2) {
            for (int i=0; i<size; i++)
              value += a1[i] + a2[i];
          }
        }
      }
      return value;
    }
```

The synchronized method modifier is removed and replaced with two synch-ronized statements in the body of the method. Instead of the sumArrays method synchronizing on the object on which the method was invoked, this method syn-chronizes on the objects it accesses. As this code is now written, the arrays are unable to be changed by another thread during the summation loop. Locking mul-tiple objects, however, can create deadlock. See PRAXIS 52 for a discussion of deadlock and how to avoid it.

When using synchronization, keep in mind what the synchronized keyword does. Understanding the fact that it locks objects—and not methods or code—results in code that behaves properly and does not fall victim to these types of errors.

PRAXIS 52: **Acquire multiple locks in a fixed, global order to avoid deadlock**

Deadlock occurs when two or more threads are blocked while waiting for each other. For example, the first thread is blocked on the second thread, waiting for a resource that the second thread holds. The second thread does not release this resource until it acquires a resource held by the first thread. Because the first thread cannot release its resource until it acquires one from the second thread, and the second thread cannot release its resource until it acquires one from the first thread, the threads are deadlocked.

Deadlock is one of the most difficult problems to handle in multithreaded code. Finding and fixing it is arduous and time consuming because it can occur in the least expected places. For example, consider the following code that locks multi-ple objects. (This is the same code from PRAXIS 51.)

```
public int sumArrays(int[] a1, int[] a2)
{
  int value = 0;
  int size = a1.length;
  if (size == a2.length) {
    synchronized(a1) {                                    //1
      synchronized(a2) {                                  //2
        for (int i=0; i<size; i++)
          value += a1[i] + a2[i];
      }
    }
  }
  return value;
}
```

This code properly locks the two array objects before they are accessed in a summation operation. It is short, simple, and properly written for the task it performs, but unfortunately it potentially has a problem. The problem is that it creates a potential deadlock situation unless additional care is taken in how this method is invoked on the same objects from different threads. To see the potential deadlock, consider the following sequence of events:

1. Two array objects are created, ArrayA and ArrayB.

2. Thread 1 invokes the sumArrays method with the following invocation: sumArrays(ArrayA, ArrayB);

3. Thread 2 invokes the sumArrays method with the following invocation: sumArrays(ArrayB, ArrayA);

4. Thread 1 begins executing the sumArrays method and acquires the lock for parameter a1 at //1, which for this invocation is the lock for the ArrayA object.

5. Thread 1 is then preempted before acquiring the lock for ArrayB at //2.

6. Thread 2 begins executing the sumArrays method and acquires the lock for parameter a1 at //1, which for this invocation is the lock for the ArrayB object.

7. Thread 2 then attempts to acquire the lock for parameter a2 at //2, which is the lock for the ArrayA object. Thread 2 blocks because this lock is currently held by Thread 1.

8. Thread 1 begins executing and attempts to acquire the lock for parameter a2 at //2, which is the lock for the ArrayB object. Thread 1 blocks because this lock is currently held by Thread 2.

9. Both threads are now deadlocked.

One way to avoid this problem is for code to acquire locks in a fixed, global order. In this example, if thread 1 and thread 2 call the sumArrays method with the parameters in the same order, the deadlock will not occur. This technique, however, requires programmers of multithreaded code to be careful in how they invoke methods that lock objects passed as parameters. Application of such a technique might seem unreasonable until you encounter this type of deadlock and have to debug it.

Alternatively, you can have the lock ordering embedded within the object. This allows code to query the object it is about to acquire a lock for to determine the proper locking order. As long as all objects to be locked support the lock ordering notion and code that acquires locks adheres to this strategy, you avoid these potential deadlock situations.

The disadvantage of embedded lock ordering in objects is the extra memory and runtime costs associated with its implementation. In addition, applying this technique in the previous example requires a wrapper object on the arrays to contain the lock ordering information. For example, consider the previous modified code with an implementation of the lock ordering technique:

```java
class ArrayWithLockOrder
{
  private static long num_locks = 0;
  private long lock_order;
  private int[] arr;

  public ArrayWithLockOrder(int[] a)
  {
    arr = a;
    synchronized(ArrayWithLockOrder.class) {
      num_locks++;              //Increment the number of locks.
      lock_order = num_locks;   //Set the unique lock_order for
    }                           //this object instance.
  }
  public long lockOrder()
  {
    return lock_order;
  }
  public int[] array()
  {
    return arr;
  }
}
```

```
class SomeClass implements Runnable
{
  //...
  public int sumArrays(ArrayWithLockOrder a1,
                       ArrayWithLockOrder a2)
  {
    int value = 0;
    ArrayWithLockOrder first = a1;   //Keep a local copy of array
    ArrayWithLockOrder last = a2;    //references.
    int size = a1.array().length;
    if (size == a2.array().length)
    {
      if (a1.lockOrder() > a2.lockOrder()) //Determine and set the
      {                                    //lock order of the
        first = a2;                        //objects.
        last = a1;
      }
      synchronized(first) {  //Lock the objects in correct order.
        synchronized(last) {
          for (int i=0; i<size; i++)
            value += (a1.array())[i] + (a2.array())[i];
        }
      }
    }
    return value;
  }
  public void run()
  {
    //...
  }
}
```

The ArrayWithLockOrder class is provided as a wrapper to the arrays used in the first example. This class increments the static num_locks variable each time a new object of the class is created. A separate lock_order instance variable is set to the current value of the num_locks static variable. This ensures that each object of this class has a unique value for the lock_order variable. The lock_order instance variable serves as the indicator for the order that this object should be locked in relation to other objects of this class.

Note that the manipulation of the static num_locks variable is done from within a synchronized statement. This is required because each instance of an object shares its static variables. Therefore, if two threads create an object of the ArrayWithLockOrder class concurrently, the static num_locks variable could be corrupted if the code manipulating it is not synchronized. Synchronizing this code ensures that each object of the ArrayWithLockOrder class has a unique value for its lock_order variable.

The `sumArrays` method is also updated to include code to determine the correct lock ordering. Before locks are requested, each object is queried for its lock order. Lower numbers are locked first. This code ensures that regardless of the order in which objects are passed to this method, they are always locked in the same order.

The `static num_locks` field and `lock_order` field are both implemented as a `long`. The `long` data type is implemented as a 64-bit signed two's complement integer. This means that the `num_locks` and `lock_order` values will roll over after 9,223,372,036,854,775,807 objects are created. It is unlikely that you will reach this limit, but it is possible under the right circumstances.

Implementing embedded lock ordering requires some extra work, memory, and execution time. However, you might find it worth the cost if these types of deadlock situations are possible in your code. If you cannot afford the extra memory and execution overhead or the likelihood exists of rolling over the `num_locks` or `lock_order` fields, you should carefully establish a predefined order for locking objects.

PRAXIS 53: Prefer `notifyAll` to `notify`

Previous PRAXES in this section discuss object locks and synchronization and the various issues surrounding them. Synchronization allows threads to cooperate with one another by not accessing the same objects at the same time. Java also allows for event notification. This is needed when one or more threads is waiting for a specific event to occur.

Java provides the `wait`, `notify`, and `notifyAll` methods to facilitate event notification. The `notify` and `notifyAll` methods are used to wake up threads that are in a wait state. (Threads enter a wait state by calling the `wait` method.) How do `notify` and `notifyAll` differ, and when should you use one over the other?

The `notify` method wakes up only one thread. This is advantageous when you know only one thread is waiting. The problem with `notify` is that when more than one thread is waiting, you cannot predict, or specify, which waiting thread wakes up. The thread chosen by the JVM is out of your control. The JVM does not necessarily choose a higher-priority thread over a lower-priority thread when choosing which thread to wake up.

Assume three threads are waiting on a particular object lock. One of the threads is waiting on the value of a `boolean` variable to change from `false` to `true`. The code that changes the value of the `boolean` variable then issues a call to the `notify` method. The `notify` method wakes up only one thread. Because three threads are waiting, the thread that is awakened might not be the thread that is interested in this particular state change. Therefore, the thread that is waiting for this state change is never notified.

Use of the `notify` method is safe under two conditions:

1. When only one thread is waiting, thus guaranteeing it is awakened

2. When multiple threads are waiting on the same condition and it does not matter which thread is awakened

By contrast, the `notifyAll` method wakes up all waiting threads. Using `notifyAll` guarantees that if you have a thread that is waiting on a condition, it is awakened. In the previous example, if the code that changes the value of the `boolean` variable calls the `notifyAll` method, all threads waiting are awakened.

Therefore, except for the two conditions listed previously, using the `notifyAll` method is better because it guarantees that all waiting threads are awakened. Remember that awakening all threads does not mean they all acquire the lock. It simply means they all return from the call to the `wait` method to retest their wait condition.

Unfortunately, the `notifyAll` method, like the `notify` method, does not provide a way to specify the order in which waiting threads are notified. The order depends on the JVM, and no guarantees are made beyond the fact that all waiting threads are awakened. Threads are not necessarily notified in their priority order. This presents a problem when you need to notify multiple threads in a particular order.

To solve this problem, you must implement the solution yourself. A general solution is available, called the "Specific Notification Pattern."[2] This pattern is described in the book, *Concurrent Programming in Java*™.[3] The specific notification pattern is very useful in that it allows you to control the order in which threads are notified.

---

[2] The "Specific Notification Pattern" was developed by Tom Cargill. A paper on this pattern with code examples of its use are at http://www.sni.net/~cargill/jgf/9809/SpecificNotification.html.

[3] *Concurrent Programming in Java*™, Doug Lea, Addison-Wesley, 1997.

A point previously made about threads, `notify`, and `notifyAll` must be stressed. The priority of a thread does not determine whether it is notified (in the case of using the `notify` method) or in what order multiple threads are notified (in the case of using the `notifyAll` method). Therefore, you should never make assumptions about the order in which threads are awakened as a result of calls to these methods. In addition, you should never make assumptions about the scheduling of a thread during preemption. Thread scheduling is implementation-dependent and varies by platform. It is unwise to make this type of assumption if your code is to be portable.

PRAXIS 54: Use spin locks for `wait` and `notifyAll`

When synchronizing multiple threads that access common data, you often need to use a notification mechanism with the `wait` and `notifyAll` methods. Using these methods requires the application of the spin-lock pattern so that your code works properly.

To illustrate, consider code that implements a robot controller. The RobotController class controls the actions of various robots connected to a computer. The controller and robots all run on separate threads. The controller provides a table of commands that is stored in a `static commands` field of the Robot class. Any robot can execute the commands. When a robot is finished executing the commands, it sets the `commands` variable to `null` and waits for more commands from the controller.

The robots wait for commands by a call to the `wait` method on the controller object. When the data arrives, they perform the commands in the table and then return to the wait state. The code for the controller and two robots might look like this:

```
class Robot extends Thread
{
  private static byte[] commands;
  private RobotController controller;
  public Robot(RobotController c)
  {
    controller = c;
  }
  public static void storeCommands(byte[] b)
  {
    commands = b;
  }
```

```
    public void processCommand(byte b)
    {
      //Move the robot based on the command.
    }

    public void run()
    {
      while(true)
      {
        synchronized(controller) {                              //1
          if (commands == null)                                 //2
          {
            try {
              controller.wait();                                //3
            }
            catch(InterruptedException e){}  //Exception is ignored
          }                                  //purposefully.
          //Now we have commands for the robot.
          int size = commands.length;
          for (int i=0; i<size; i++)
            processCommand(commands[i]);     //Move the robot.
          commands = null;
        }
      }
    }
}

class RobotController extends Thread
{
    private Robot robot1;
    private Robot robot2;
    public static void main(String args[])
    {
      RobotController rc = new RobotController();
      rc.start();
    }

    public void run()
    {
      robot1 = new Robot(this);
      robot1.start();
      robot2 = new Robot(this);
      robot2.start();
    }

    public void loadCommands(byte[] b)
    {
      synchronized(this) {                                      //4
        Robot.storeCommands(b);  //Give the commands to the Robot
        notifyAll();             //class. Notify all threads.
```

```
        }
      }
    }
```

Notice that the `run` method of the `Robot` class first acquires the lock for the `RobotController` object at //1. This is done so the `Robot` objects can operate on the table of commands without the `RobotController` object changing it. Note that the `loadCommands` method of the `RobotController` class, at //4, acquires the same object lock. These `synchronized` blocks ensure the robot command table is not altered when it is in use.

After the lock is acquired at //1, the `Robot` code then checks to see if there is a table of robot commands to process at //2. If such a table does not exist, the code executes a call to `wait` on the `RobotController` object at //3. This call releases the lock acquired at //1 and goes into a wait state. When the `loadCommands` method of the `RobotController` class is called, a `notifyAll` is issued, thereby waking up all of the `Robot` threads. To run, each thread must first reacquire the `RobotController` object lock. Only one thread acquires this lock at a time; the others must wait. The `Robot` thread that gets the lock can now access the table of commands and move the robot accordingly.

This code has a bug that causes it to fail in certain situations. Consider the following sequence of events:

1. An object of the `RobotController` class is created along with two objects of the `Robot` class. Each object runs on its own thread.

2. The first `Robot` thread checks to see whether the `commands` variable is `null` at //2.

3. The `commands` variable is `null`, so the first `Robot` thread blocks at //3 with a call to `wait`.

4. The second `Robot` thread checks to see whether the `commands` variable is `null` at //2.

5. The `commands` variable is `null`, so the second `Robot` thread blocks at //3 with a call to `wait`.

6. The `loadCommands` method of the `RobotController` class is called with a table of commands.

7. The loadCommands method calls the notifyAll method.

8. Both Robot threads are unblocked and attempt to reacquire the RobotController object lock.

9. Because only one thread can acquire the lock, assume the lock is obtained by the first Robot thread. The second Robot thread does not acquire the lock until the first Robot thread releases it.

10. The first Robot thread processes the commands for the robot, sets the commands variable to null, and releases the lock.

11. The second Robot thread acquires the lock and attempts to process the commands for the robot.

12. Because the commands variable is null, the code fails with a NullPointerException.

The problem with this code is that it failed to recheck the value of the commands variable before proceeding. Because all threads are awakened on a call to notifyAll, they all eventually reacquire the object lock in an undetermined order (see PRAXIS 53). When they reacquire the lock and begin execution, they start at the line of code immediately following the call to the wait method. When a thread is awakened, it must recheck the condition on which it was waiting. This is because it might not be the first thread to run and the condition could have changed.

In the previous example, the first thread that runs changes the value of the condition variable. The first thread sets the commands field to null. Because the code does not recheck the value of the commands variable, the second thread fails. Whenever code is waiting on a particular condition, it should do so inside of a loop or a spin lock. The correct implementation of the run method of the Robot class is as follows:

```
public void run()
{
  while(true)
  {
    synchronized(controller) {
      while (commands == null)                                   //1
      {
        try {
          controller.wait();
        }
        catch(InterruptedException e){}   //Exception is ignored
      }                                   //purposefully.
```

```
      //Now we have commands for the robot.
      int size = commands.length;
      for (int i=0; i<size; i++)
        processCommand(commands[i]);  //Move the robot.
      commands = null;
    }
  }
}
```

The only line of code changed is the line at //1—the `if (commands == null)` is changed to a `while` loop. According to this code, each thread that is awakened retests the condition it is waiting on before proceeding. Each thread checks to see whether the `commands` variable is still non-`null` before accessing it. This is to be sure that a thread that was awakened earlier did not change the value of this variable.

Notice that the `InterruptedException` thrown by the `wait` method is ignored. It is typically a bad idea to ignore an exception. (For more on this topic, see PRAXIS 17.) However, this case can be an exception to that rule. You can choose to ignore the exception when the thread is interrupted because with a spin lock, the code will retest the condition. If the condition is not satisfied, the thread will reenter the wait state by calling `wait`. If an `InterruptedException` signals an error in your design, you should not ignore this exception.

Spin locks are a simple and cheap way to ensure proper behavior and execution of code that waits on condition variables. However, if you forget to use them, then your code might work some of the time, but when the timing of the threads is just so, your code will fail. Code that fails occasionally represents some of the more difficult bugs to track down. The utilization of spin locks removes this potential bug.

PRAXIS 55: Use `wait` and `notifyAll` instead of polling loops

Before the advent of more advanced communication mechanisms, programmers relied on other techniques to communicate between different parts of a system. One commonly used technique was the *polling loop*.

A *polling loop* consists of code in one thread that sits in a loop and continually tests a particular condition. The condition the polling thread waits on is ultimately changed by another thread. When the condition is satisfied, the code performs some task. If the condition is not satisfied, the code might sleep for a brief amount of time and then test the condition again. For example, consider the following code that uses polling to wait until data has been provided in a pipe:

```
class ReadFromPipe extends Thread
{
  private Pipe pipe;

  //...
  public void run()
  {
    int data;
    while(true)
    {
      while((data = pipe.getData()) == 0)
      {
        //No data, so sleep for a while and try again.
        try {
          sleep(200);
        }
        catch(InterruptedException e){}   //Exception is ignored
      }                                   //purposefully.
      synchronized(pipe) {
        //Process data
      }
    }
  }
}
```

An object of the `ReadFromPipe` class runs on a separate thread and performs polling. The `run` method contains an infinite loop that continually queries the `Pipe` class to see if any data is available to be read. If there is no data, the thread sleeps for `200` milliseconds and then queries again.

This code works, but it is inefficient because the polling loop takes up processor cycles. When there is no data in the pipe, this thread still requires processor cycles to query the pipe for data.

A more efficient implementation uses the `wait` method with `notify` or `notifyAll`. Proper use of these methods eliminates the need to waste processor cycles on polling. For example, the previous code rewritten to avoid polling and use `wait` and `notifyAll` looks like this:

```
class ReadFromPipe extends Thread
{
  private Pipe pipe;
  //...
```

```
public void run()
{
  int data;
  while(true)
  {
    synchronized(pipe) {
      while((data = pipe.getData()) == 0)
      {
        try {
          pipe.wait();                                    //1
        }
        catch(InterruptedException e){}  //Exception is ignored
      }                                  //purposefully.
      //Process data
    }
  }
}
```

The advantage of this code is the call to pipe.wait at //1. When the wait method is called, the object lock for the pipe object is released and the thread is suspended. The suspended thread does not use any processor cycles. It remains suspended until either it is awakened by a call to notify or notifyAll (see PRAXIS 53) or it is interrupted. When the thread is awakened, it rechecks its condition (see PRAXIS 54). If the condition is such that there is still no data, the thread invokes pipe.wait again and remains suspended until it is awakened. Otherwise, the thread performs its processing based on the received data.

PRAXIS 34 discusses the high cost of synchronization. These costs should not lead programmers to shun synchronization in favor of polling loops. Polling loops are much more inefficient than synchronized code. For example, running the previous two code samples results in the synchronized code's performing many orders of magnitude faster than the code implemented with polling. Therefore, you should avoid polling whenever possible. (See PRAXIS 58 for one case where you must use polling.)

Remove polling loops from your code and replace them with spin locks that use the wait, notify, and notifyAll methods. This will make your code much more efficient. These methods allow a thread that is waiting for data to be suspended instead of continually polling and unnecessarily using processor cycles.

PRAXIS 56:   **Do not reassign the object reference of a locked object**

PRAXIS 46 explains that the synchronized keyword locks objects. Because the object is locked inside of synchronized code, what does that mean to the object and to changes you make to its object reference? Synchronizing on an object locks only the object. You must be careful, however, not to reassign an object reference of a locked object. What happens if you do? Consider the following code that implements a stack:

```java
class Stack
{
  private int stackSize = 10;
  private int[] intArr = new int[stackSize];
  private int index;  //Next available slot in the stack.

  public void push(int val)
  {
    synchronized(intArr) {
      //Reallocate integer array(our stack) if it is full.
      if (index == intArr.length)
      {
        stackSize *= 2;
        int[] newintArr = new int[stackSize];
        System.arraycopy(intArr, 0 , newintArr, 0, intArr.length);
        intArr = newintArr;
      }
      intArr[index] = val;
      index++;
    }
  }

  public int pop()
  {
    int retval;
    synchronized(intArr) {
      if (index > 0)
      {
        retval = intArr[index-1];  //Retrieve the value, and
        index--;                   //decrement the stack.
        return retval;
      }
    }
    throw new EmptyStackException();
  }
  //...
}
```

194

This code implements a stack in terms of an array. An array with an initial size of 10 is created to hold integer values. The class implements the push and pop methods to simulate stack usage. In the push method, if no more room exists in the array to hold the value that is pushed, then the array is reallocated to create additional storage. (This class is intentionally not implemented with a Vector. You cannot store primitive types in a Vector. For additional information on arrays and Vectors, see PRAXES 4 and 41).

Notice that this code is intended to be accessed by multiple threads. Each access of the shared instance data of the class by the push and pop methods is done within a synchronized block. This ensures that multiple threads cannot access the array concurrently and thereby generate incorrect results.

This code has a major flaw. It synchronizes on the integer array object, referenced by intArr, of the Stack class. This flaw surfaces when the push method reallocates the integer array. When this occurs, the object reference, intArr, is reassigned to refer to a new, larger, integer array object. Notice that this occurs during the execution of the push method's synchronized block. This block is synchronized on the object referenced by the intArr variable. Therefore, the object that is locked inside of this code is no longer being used. Consider the following sequence of events:

1. Thread 1 calls the push method and acquires the intArr object lock.

2. Thread 1 is preempted by thread 2.

3. Thread 2 calls the pop method. This method blocks because it attempts to acquire the same lock that is currently held by thread 1 in the push method.

4. Thread 1 regains control and reallocates the array. The intArr variable now references a different object.

5. The push method exits and releases its lock for the original intArr object.

6. Thread 1 calls the push method again and acquires the lock for the new intArr object.

7. Thread 1 is preempted by thread 2.

8. Thread 2 acquires the object lock for the old intArr object and attempts to access its memory.

Now thread 1 has a lock for the new object referred to by intArr and thread 2 has a lock for the old object referred to by intArr. Because both threads hold different locks, they can execute the synchronized push and pop methods concurrently and thereby generate errors. Clearly, this is not what is intended.

This problem is caused by the push method's reassigning the object reference of an object that is locked. When an object is locked, the possibility exists that other threads are blocked on the same object lock. If you reassign the object reference of the locked object to another object, then the pending locks of other threads are on an object that is no longer relevant in the code.

You fix this code by removing synchronization of the intArr variable and synchronizing the push and pop methods. Do this by adding the synchronized keyword as a method modifier. The correct code looks like this:

```
class Stack
{
  //As before...
  public synchronized void push(int val)
  {
    //Reallocate integer array(our stack) if it is full.
    if (index == intArr.length)
    {
      stackSize *= 2;
      int[] newintArr = new int[stackSize];
      System.arraycopy(intArr, 0 , newintArr, 0, intArr.length);
      intArr = newintArr;
    }
    intArr[index] = val;
    index++;
  }

  public synchronized int pop()
  {
    int retval;
    if (index > 0)
    {
      retval = intArr[index-1];
      index--;
      return retval;
    }
    throw new EmptyStackException();
  }
}
```

This modification changes the actual lock acquired. Instead of the object referenced by the intArr variable being locked, the lock obtained is that for the object on which the method was invoked. This allows the code to reassign the intArr object reference because the lock acquired is no longer on the object to which `intArr` refers.

PRAXIS 57: **Do not invoke the `stop` or `suspend` methods**

The `stop` and `suspend` methods are both deprecated in the Java 2 SDK. Deprecated methods are no longer supported and might be removed from future releases. Methods that are deprecated are sometimes replaced with alternative methods. Other times, they are not replaced because they are inherently unsafe. The `stop` and `suspend` methods are both unsafe and currently do not have replacements.

Although they are deprecated in the Java 2 SDK, they still contain an implementation and an API. They can, therefore, still be invoked. But using these methods creates more problems than they solve. Avoid them.

The `stop` method was intended as a means of stopping a thread's execution. The problem with stopping a thread is not with object locks but with object state. When a thread is stopped with the `stop` method, all locks held by the thread are released. However, you do not know what the code in the thread is doing at the time it is stopped. For example, consider a thread that writes data into a shared memory buffer. The shared memory buffer is represented by an object. If you want to stop this thread by invoking its `stop` method, how do you know that the thread is finished with its current write operation? The fact is, you do not know. If the thread is abruptly stopped, the object that represents the shared memory buffer might not be in a valid state. Therefore, another thread that accesses the shared memory buffer will access invalid data.

You can safely use the `stop` method if you are careful. If you know that at the time you call it the thread you are stopping is not actively updating or processing other objects or data, then you can safely use `stop`. However, these cases are rare. In addition, you might think you are safely invoking `stop` when in fact it is not safe to do so. Because of these issues, the `stop` method was deemed unsafe and was deprecated.

So, how do you stop the execution of a thread? Because there is no direct replacement for the `stop` method, you must use some type of thread cooperation. PRAXIS 58 discusses this and offers an example of how to safely stop a thread.

The suspend method was intended as a means of temporarily suspending a thread. (There is a corresponding resume method that resumed a previously suspended thread. The resume method has also been deprecated.) The suspend method is also unsafe but for a different reason than that concerning the stop method.

Unlike the stop method, the suspend method does not release the locks held by the thread before suspending. These locks cannot be released until the thread resumes execution.

Suppose a thread that is to resume a suspended thread requests a lock that is currently held by the suspended thread. A good design would negate this problem, but it is possible nonetheless. Remember, when a thread is suspended it does not release any locks it currently holds. This sequence of events results in deadlock. Because the thread that holds the lock is suspended and the thread that is to call the resume method is waiting on the lock held by the suspended thread, a deadlock results. Because of this problem, the suspend and resume methods were deemed unsafe and were deprecated.

The Java API has another method that, at first glance, looks like it might safely stop a thread: destroy. This method is part of the java.lang.Thread class but is currently not implemented. The documentation for this method indicates that if it is implemented, it will suffer from the same problems as suspend. If it is implemented in a future release, carefully analyze exactly what it does. Chances are that its implementation will not be a safe way to stop a thread's execution.

Avoid using the stop and suspend methods. The stop method risks internal corruption of data, and the suspend method risks deadlock. Both cause unpredictable and incorrect behavior. Multithreaded programming is complex enough. Do not make it more complex by using methods that elicit these types of problems.

PRAXIS 58: Terminate threads through thread cooperation

PRAXIS 57 advises against using the stop method to terminate a thread. PRAXIS 55 advises against using polling loops. Because there is no replacement for the stop method, you must find other means to safely terminate a thread's execution. Unfortunately, the solution requires a polling loop.

A thread terminates when its run method exits. To safely stop a thread, you need a mechanism to gracefully exit the run method of the thread you want to stop. One option is to provide a variable in the class, and a method that sets it, to indicate when a thread should be stopped. You might implement this technique like this:

```
class Test extends Thread
{
  private boolean stop;

  public void stopThread()
  {
    stop = true;
  }

  public void run()
  {
    while(!stop)
    {
      //Do work...
    }
    //Clean up...
  }
}
```

This design attempts to allow a thread to be gracefully stopped. However, it has a problem described shortly. In the run method, the code checks to see if it has been requested to be stopped by itself or another thread each time through its loop. If so, it can perform any cleanup and exit its run method, thereby terminating the thread.

One drawback to this solution is the potential unwanted delay involved to stop a thread. Consider that thread 1 calls the stopThread method on thread 2. Thread 2 might be inside of its while loop, performing some task, and might not loop back to check its stop variable in a timely fashion. This technique has the advantage that the thread, when requested to stop, can do so on its own terms. Thus, it has the opportunity to perform any necessary cleanup before exiting.

The previous code is not totally correct. The problem is with the stop variable. When the stop variable is set to true in the stopThread method, the code in the run method is not guaranteed to see the changed value. This problem exists because Java allows threads to keep copies of variables from main memory in the private working memory of the thread. This is done as a performance optimization. Access to a variable is more efficient when performed on private working memory than when performed in main memory. For more on private and working memory and issues surrounding it, see PRAXIS 50.

Two ways are available to ensure that the private working copy of a variable is reconciled with the copy in main memory:

1. Perform the access in a `synchronized` method or block.

2. Declare the variable `volatile`.

When code enters and leaves a `synchronized` method or block, the variables the code accesses are copied from and to main memory. This ensures the values of the variables are accurate and that they reflect any changes that took place to them from other threads.

In the previous example, accessing the `stop` variable is not done within a `synchronized` method or block. If you do not want to add synchronization, you can use the second option.

Declaring variables `volatile` forces the Java runtime to reconcile the private working copy of the variable with main memory each time the variable is accessed. Declaring the `stop` variable `volatile` ensures its value is up-to-date and accurate with regard to any other thread changing it. Modifying the code with the `volatile` keyword looks like this:

```
class Test extends Thread
{
  private volatile boolean stop;

  public void stopThread()
  {
    stop = true;
  }

  public void run()
  {
    while(!stop)
    {
      //Do work...
    }
    //Clean up...
  }
}
```

Until a safe replacement for the `stop` method is provided, you must use a technique like this to safely stop threads. This technique requires threads to cooperate so that they can be stopped gracefully while maintaining object state.

Classes and Interfaces

All the world over, I will back the masses against the classes.
—William Ewart Gladstone

CLASSES are at the core of all software written in Java. The structure and design of a class define how the class behaves, as well as how it is used. Java provides three constructs to express classes, their interfaces, and their behavior: class, abstract class, and interface. This section gives examples and advice concerning the selection and use of each.

The term *interface* relates both to the notion of an interface declaration and to the generic notion of the interface that a class exposes through its methods. In this regard, understanding object finalization and immutability is critical when designing and implementing properly behaved classes. You should be careful when relying on object finalization for non-memory resource cleanup. You also should understand the various issues and available techniques for defining classes that produce immutable objects. This section examines these and other issues.

PRAXIS 59: Use interfaces to support multiple inheritance

Java often is said not to support multiple inheritance. In fact, it does not support one common notion of multiple inheritance—multiple inheritance of implementation. It does, however, support multiple inheritance of interface.

To understand how these two notions of multiple inheritance differ, consider a set of classes for a vehicle and its value. You might represent the vehicle, its value, and an implementation by using multiple Java class declarations. This design is a mistake, however, as the following classes demonstrate:

```
class Vehicle
{
  //Methods of a Vehicle
}

class Asset
{
  //Methods of an asset
}

class MyCar extends Vehicle, Asset
{
  //...
}
```

Attempting to compile this code results in:

```
MyCar.java:1: Multiple inheritance is not supported.
class MyCar extends Vehicle, Asset
                    ^
1 error
```

Multiple inheritance of implementation would be accomplished by extending more than one class, as is attempted here. This is explicitly disallowed in Java, however, thereby leading many to say Java does not support multiple inheritance.

Java does, however, provide the `interface` declaration. Like a class, an `interface` declares a reference type. The declaration of an `interface` represents the signatures and intended behavior of methods. An `interface` cannot contain any implementation and, therefore, cannot require specific behavior. However, the return type and signature of each method in an `interface` describe its intended behavior.

With an `interface`, Java supports the notion of multiple inheritance, specifically, multiple inheritance of `interface`. That is, a Java class may extend no more than one class, but it may implement multiple interfaces.

Consider the same requirement for designing a set of classes for a vehicle and its value. You can represent various common interfaces for a vehicle by using multiple Java `interface` declarations. Concrete classes can then implement one or more interfaces to support the different types of behavior implied by the `interface`. Consider the following `interface` declarations:

```
interface Vehicle
{
  public void startEngine();
  public void stopEngine();
  public void accelerate();
  public void decelerate();
}

interface Asset
{
  public int initialCost();
  public int currentValue();
  public double rateOfGrowth();
}
```

Now consider a concrete class implementation of the Vehicle interface:

```
class MyCar implements Vehicle
{
  public void startEngine() {
    //Code to start engine...
  }
  public void stopEngine() {
    //Code to stop engine...
  }
  public void accelerate()  {
    //Code to accelerate...
  }
  public void decelerate() {
    //Code to decelerate...
  }
  public void loadPeopleInCar() {
    //Code to load people in car...
  }
  public int adultSeating() {
    return 2;
  }
  public int childSeating() {
    return 2;
  }
}
```

The MyCar class is a concrete implementation of the Vehicle interface. To be a concrete implementation a class must provide implementations for the methods defined in the Vehicle interface. This class implements those methods as well as provides three methods of its own: loadPeopleInCar, adultSeating, and childSeating.

Now assume you want to create another car class that is both a Vehicle and an Asset. Because Vehicle and Asset are interfaces, you can do this. For example:

```java
class PassengerCar implements Vehicle, Asset
{
  public void startEngine() {
    //Code to start engine...
  }
  public void stopEngine() {
    //Code to stop engine...
  }
  public void accelerate()  {
    //Code to accelerate...
  }
  public void decelerate() {
    //Code to decelerate...
  }
  public int initialCost() {
    //Return initialCost...
  }
  public int currentValue() {
    //Calculate and return current value...
  }
  public double rateOfGrowth() {
    //Calculate and return the growth rate of the car...
    //For most cars, this will be negative.
  }
  public void loadPeopleInCar() {
    //Code to load people in car...
  }
  public int adultSeating() {
    return 4;
  }
  public int childSeating() {
    return 3;
  }
}
```

The PassengerCar class implements two interfaces. When implementing an interface, a class must provide implementations for all of the methods declared in the interface. The PassengerCar class also provides the loadPeopleInCar, adultSeating, and childSeating methods to provide the appropriate behavior and values for these methods for this car.

The PassengerCar class exhibits multiple inheritance of interface. Use of this type of inheritance enables other classes to implement the individual interfaces that make sense for them.

You also can use the interface declaration as a *marker interface*. A marker interface is an interface without any methods. It is used to signal that any class that implements the marker interface has some property.

For example, one marker interface in the Java class libraries is the Serializable interface. This interface contains no methods, but classes that implement it are expected to exhibit serializing properties. Marker interfaces should provide sufficient documentation to indicate what properties a class that implements the interface should exhibit. Therefore, if you implement a marker interface you know how to code your class so that the properties prescribed by the marker interface are coded properly.

To test whether a class implements a marker interface, use the instanceof operator. For example:

```
import java.io.*;
class Foo implements Serializable
{
  //...
}

//...
Foo somefoo = new Foo();
if (somefoo instanceof Serializable)
//...
```

Remember, an interface, like a class, declares a reference type. Therefore, an object of a class that implements an interface is an instance of that interface type. For example, the previous PassengerCar class implements the Vehicle interface and the Asset interface. Therefore, an object of the PassengerCar class is an instance of Vehicle and Asset. Consider the following code:

```
PassengerCar pcar = new PassengerCar();
if (pcar instanceof Vehicle)                              //True
  //...
if (pcar instanceof Asset)                                //True
  //...
```

In summary, use interfaces to support single and multiple inheritance or when implementing a marker interface. Interfaces are limited to public methods and constants and may not contain any implementation. This makes an interface an expression of a contract to be implemented by a concrete class. Although classes can extend only one other class, interfaces allow classes to implement various interface declarations. This represents the multiple inheritance of interface that Java supports.

PRAXIS 60: Avoid method clashes in interfaces

Nothing prevents two interfaces from using the same names for constants or declaring methods with the same name or signature. This can cause problems for a class that implements two or more interfaces that have these characteristics. Consider the following interface declarations for a golfer and a bowler:

```
interface Golfer
{
    public static final int HighScore = 90;
    public static final int LowScore = 72;
    public int computeScore();
}

interface Bowler
{
    public static int HighScore = 300;
    public static int LowScore = 120;
    public void computeScore();
}
```

Given these two interface declarations, a class may not legally implement both. The computeScore methods of each interface, although having the same signatures, differ in their return types.[1] Therefore, compiling any class that attempts to implement both results in a compiler error. For example:

```
class Enthusiast implements Golfer, Bowler
{
    public void computeScore()
    {
        //...
    }
}
```

Compiling this class results in the following output from the compiler:

---

[1] The return type is not part of a method's signature.

206

```
Enthusiast.java:3: The method void computeScore() declared in
class Enthusiast cannot override the method of the same signature
declared in interface Golfer.  They must have the same return
type.
   public void computeScore()
                 ^
1 error
```

If you have access to the source code for these interfaces, you can attempt to fix
this problem by matching the return types of the methods. For example:

```
interface Golfer
{
  public static final int HighScore = 90;
  public static final int LowScore = 72;
  public void computeScore();
}

interface Bowler
{
  public static int HighScore = 300;
  public static int LowScore = 120;
  public void computeScore();
}
```

Now consider a class that implements these two interfaces:

```
class Enthusiast implements Golfer, Bowler
{
  public void computeScore()
  {
    //...
  }
}
```

Because both `interface` declarations each provide a method with the same signature and return type, the `Enthusiast` class compiles cleanly. Furthermore, you
might notice that each `interface` declares two constants that have the same
name. This is not a problem. To access the constants from the `Enthusiast` class,
refer to them with their qualified names. For example:

```
int golfLowScore = Golfer.LowScore;
int bowlingLowScore = Bowler.LowScore;
```

The problem you now have is one of semantics. When you implement the computeScore method of the `Enthusiast` class, which score do you compute? The

semantics of the computeScore method implementation for golf are completely different from those for bowling. What the implementation should be is unclear.

If the method had a generic implementation, this would not be a problem. In this case, however, no one correct way exists to implement the computeScore method for both a Golfer and a Bowler.

If you have access to the source code for these interfaces and are able to change them, you can easily eliminate this problem. Assuming you do not have the source, you might resort to other means. You might, for example, define another interface that extends the existing Golfer interface. This interface declares a new method that does not conflict with the one in the Bowler interface. For example:

```
interface MyGolfer extends Golfer
{
  public void computeGolfScore();
}
```

Thus, the Enthusiast class implements this interface instead of the Golfer interface. Consider:

```
class Enthusiast implements MyGolfer, Bowler
{
  public void computeScore()
  {
    //...
  }
  public void computeGolfScore()
  {
    //...
  }
}
```

The Enthusiast class is now required to implement the computeScore method, which is found in the Bowler interface and the Golfer interface, as well as the computeGolfScore method of the MyGolfer interface. This enables the Enthusiast class to contain two distinct methods for computing the appropriate scores.

This solution, however, has a major problem. Anywhere the Golfer interface is used, the code has access only to the computeScore method and not the computeGolfScore method. This is because objects referenced through the Golfer interface type can call only methods of this interface or of any other interface it might extend. Therefore, implementing another `interface` does not solve this semantic clash problem. In this case, your best option is to forgo the Enthusiast class that is both a `Golfer` and a `Bowler` and instead implement two separate classes. For example:

```
class GolfEnthusiast implements Golfer
{
  public void computeScore()
  {
    //Compute golf score...
  }
}

class BowlingEnthusiast implements Bowler
{
  public void computeScore()
  {
    //Compute bowling score...
  }
}
```

Name clash problems are always possible, and you need to take steps to minimize them. The name clash in the preceding example could have been avoided if the methods had been named differently. For example, instead of `computeScore`, the methods could have been named, `computeGolfScore` and `computeBowling-Score`. Carefully naming methods will not eliminate every potential name clash problem, but it can minimize them. However, name clash problems are most likely encountered by programmers implementing interfaces from disjoint libraries.

In summary, an `interface` is a useful tool for programmers as they design and develop code. When defining interfaces, however, the potential for name clashes exists with methods and constants. You should name methods and constants carefully in order to minimize the likelihood of a name clash with another `interface`.

PRAXIS 61: Use `abstract` classes when it makes sense to provide a partial implementation

Java provides the ability to declare an `abstract` class. An *abstract class* is a class that cannot be instantiated but that allows methods declared within it to provide an implementation. The methods of an `abstract` class differ from methods in an `interface` in that the latter cannot provide any implementation. (For more on interfaces, see PRAXES 59, 60, and 62.)

An abstract class can define methods that provide a default implementation and methods that provide no implementation. Because all methods of an abstract class might not provide a complete implementation, creating an instance of one does not make sense. In fact, if you do attempt to create an instance of an abstract class the compiler will generate an error.

Providing an abstract class is useful when you want to declare a class and provide only part of its implementation. The part of the implementation you provide, in the methods of the abstract class, should either make sense for all objects of that class or be a default implementation. The default implementation can then be overridden by subclasses wanting different behavior for that method. Other parts of its implementation might make sense only for each derived class to provide. In this case, these methods would be left without an implementation in the abstract class.

All methods in an abstract class that do not have an implementation are abstract methods. A derived class that extends an abstract class must implement all of the class's abstract methods in order for the class to be considered concrete. A *concrete class* is a class for which objects can be created. If a class extends an abstract class but does not provide implementations for all of its abstract methods, then the new extended class is also abstract.

To demonstrate a use for an abstract class, consider the following class declaration that computes team scores in a two-player, better-ball golf match:[2]

```
abstract class TeamScores
{
  private Team team;

  public abstract int player1Score(int holeNumber, Team team);
  public abstract int player2Score(int holeNumber, Team team);
  public abstract void storeTeamScore(int score, Team team);
  public void processBetterBallTeamScores(Team team)
  {
    int teamScore = 0;
    for (int i=1; i<=18; i++)  //Compute team scores for each hole
    {
      int p1Score = player1Score(i, team);
      int p2Score = player2Score(i, team);
```

---

[2] Two-player better-ball consists of two players on the same team competing against two players on another team. Both players on each team play each hole with their own balls. A team's score for each hole is the lower of the two scores. This format is also called Four-Ball.

```
        if (p1Score < p2Score)
          teamScore = p1Score;
        else
          teamScore = p2Score;
        storeTeamScore(teamScore, team);
    }
  }
}
```

The TeamScores class is declared abstract because part of its implementation is the same for all derived classes whereas other parts need to be provided by each derived class. This class is used to compute the better-ball scores of two-player teams. The algorithm to compute the team scores is the same regardless of the teams and the scores. Therefore, the implementation for the processBetter-BallTeamScores method can be provided in the abstract class. Other methods, such as those for players' individual scores, need to be provided by derived classes. For example, a derived class might be implemented like this:

```
class Result extends TeamScores
{
  public int player1Score(int holeNum, Team team)
  {
    int score;
    //score = lookup holeNum score for player1 on given team
    return score;
  }

  public int player2Score(int holeNum, Team team)
  {
    int score;
    //score = lookup holeNum score for player2 on given team
    return score;
  }

  public void storeTeamScore(int score, Team team)
  {
    //Store score for team...
  }
}
```

The Result class extends the abstract TeamScores class and provides implementations for all of its abstract methods. The Result class is not limited to the implementation of the methods in the TeamScores class. For example, it can provide its own implementation of the processBetterBallTeamScores method by overriding this method.

As shown, `abstract` classes are useful when you want to provide a class with a partial implementation, for example, because it is likely to be common for all derived classes. The methods that are not implemented, and thereby remain `abstract`, do not make sense to be implemented by the base class and must be provided by a derived class.

PRAXIS 62: Differentiate between an `interface`, `abstract` class, and concrete class

Deciding whether to define an `interface`, an `abstract` class, or a concrete class is often confusing. PRAXES 59 and 61 analyzed interfaces and `abstract` classes, respectively. This PRAXIS summarizes the differences between the three design choices and provides guidance on which one to choose based on your program's conditions and requirements.

The following table provides verbose descriptions of the various attributes that exist for the three design alternatives:

Table 5: Characteristics of `interfaces`, `abstract` classes, and concrete classes

	interface	abstract class	concrete class
Description	Expression of a contract without implementation.	Expression of a contract with partial implementation.	A concrete implementation, often of an `interface` or abstract class.
Use when	You want to support single or multiple `interface` inheritance or identify a marker interface.	You want to provide a class with a partial implementation.	You are providing a concrete implementation.
Contents limited to	Public methods and `public static final` constants.	Not limited.	Not limited.
Implementation	No implementation allowed.	Partial implementation allowed.	Full implementation required.

The following table briefly summarizes the major differences between `interfaces`, `abstract` classes, and concrete classes:

Table 6: Summary of `interfaces`, `abstract` classes, and concrete classes

	Enables support for multiple inheritance	Supports abstract methods	Implementation allowed	Create an instance of	Partial implementation allowed
`interface`	Y	Y[a]	N	N	N
`abstract` class	N	Y	Y	N	Y
`concrete` class	N	N	Y	Y	N

[a.] All methods of an `interface` are implicitly `abstract`. However, declaring them `abstract` results in an error when the code is compiled.

Keep this type of information in mind as you design your code in order to ensure that you use the correct constructs for the interface and contracts you express.

PRAXIS 63:   Define and implement immutable classes judiciously

Immutable objects can be a valuable and necessary construct in object-oriented programming. Sometimes you want to prohibit an object from ever being changed. By definition, an *immutable object* is an object and any object it references that does not change after construction. The object is, therefore, immutable for its lifetime. Immutable classes are commonly used to represent strings, colors, and numeric values.

Immutable objects provide a valuable service. Because they guarantee that their state cannot change after construction, they are inherently thread safe. Thread concurrency issues are relevant when one thread can change data while another thread is reading the same data. Because an immutable object never changes its data, synchronizing access to it is not needed.

Depending on the design of the immutable object, this lack of synchronization can have enormous performance benefits. (See PRAXIS 34 for a discussion on the expense of synchronization.) However, any performance gains achieved by immutable objects can be negated by the extra code you sometimes must implement to support them. For example, implementing immutable objects often requires you to implement cloning, which can be expensive. Cloning is discussed in detail in PRAXIS 64.

While immutability is a property of an object, it must be coded explicitly. There is no keyword in Java to specify immutability. However, several aspects of a class's definition and implementation enable immutability:

- Declare all data in the class `private`.

- Provide only getter methods. No setter methods are allowed.

- Declare the class `final`.

- Clone mutable objects before returning a reference to them from a getter method (see PRAXIS 64).

- Clone objects provided to the constructor that are references to mutable objects (see PRAXIS 64).

- Set all data contained in the class in the constructor.

Because an immutable object cannot be changed, all data must be declared `private`. If it is not, the data, and therefore the object, can be changed.

No setter methods are allowed because they change class data. In addition, the class must be declared `final`, to prevent its being subclassed. A subclass could provide setter methods or override one of the getter methods and return a value not consistent with the base class.

Furthermore, before a reference to any mutable object may be passed to the constructor or returned from a getter method, the object must be cloned first. If it is not, immutability can be lost (see PRAXIS 64). Because of these restrictions, all data relevant to the class's immutability must be set by the class constructor. Consider the following immutable class:

```
final class PinNumbers
{
  private String acctOwner;
  private int checkingAcctPin;
  private int savingsAcctPin;
```

```
    PinNumbers(String owner, int cPin, int sPin)
    {
      acctOwner = owner;
      checkingAcctPin = cPin;
      savingsAcctPin = sPin;
    }
    public String accountOwner()
    {
      return acctOwner;
    }
    public int checkingPin()
    {
      return checkingAcctPin;
    }
    public int savingsPin()
    {
      return savingsAcctPin;
    }
    //...
  }
```

This class is declared final to prevent subclassing. All of its data is declared private, and it provides only getter methods to access that data. Furthermore, all of the data is set by the constructor. These attributes ensure that an object of this class cannot change after it is created. You must also be sure that none of the methods for the class changes the internal data of the class and thereby break immutability.

This class does not have to clone any data because the only data types it receives in the constructor, or returns from its methods, are primitive types and object references to immutable objects. Primitive types are not objects and, therefore, cloning makes no sense for them. The String class is immutable so there is no need to clone it. PRAXIS 64 discusses the details of cloning mutable objects.

PRAXIS 64: Use clone for immutable objects when passing or receiving object references to mutable objects

When an immutable class is implemented, mutable objects passed to, or returned from, an immutable object must be properly cloned. PRAXIS 63 defines an object as immutable when it and any object it refers to do not change. If cloning is not done, then the immutability of your object is not guaranteed. Other code can retain a reference to an object in the immutable object and make changes to it, thereby breaking immutability constraints.

Consider the following class declarations: a `DiskDriveInfo` class and a `User` class. The `DiskDriveInfo` is intended to be immutable. The `User` encapsulates which user has shared access to the disk drive. The `User` object with shared access is stored as part of the `DiskDriveInfo` object. In the following example, the designer of the class was careful to make the class `final`, and all fields `private` and to provide only getter methods. Is the `DiskDriveInfo` class immutable? If not, what needs to be done to make it so?

```java
class User
{
  private String userName;
  private String userID;
  private int userNode;

  User(String name, int node)
  {
    userName = name;
    userNode = node;
  }
  public void setUserName(String name)
  {
    userName = name;
  }
  public void setUserID(String userid)
  {
    userID = userid;
  }
  public void setUserNode(int node)
  {
    userNode = node;
  }
  public String userName()
  {
    return userName;
  }
}

final class DiskDriveInfo
{
  private int driveSize;
  private String volumeLabel;
  private User driveShare;

  DiskDriveInfo(int size, String volLabel, User share)
  {
    driveSize = size;
    volumeLabel = volLabel;
    driveShare = share;
  }
```

```
     public int size()
     {
       return driveSize;
     }
     public String label()
     {
       return volumeLabel;
     }
     public User share()
     {
       return driveShare;
     }
   }
```

The `DiskDriveInfo` class is not immutable. Objects of this class can be changed. Consider the following code that creates a `DiskDriveInfo` object and tests its immutability:

```
   class Test
   {
     private static final int sizeInMeg = 200;
     public static void main(String args[])
     {
       User share1 = new User("Duke", 10);                      //1
       DiskDriveInfo dd = new DiskDriveInfo(sizeInMeg, "myDrive",
                                            share1);            //2
       User share = dd.share();
       System.out.println("User with shared access is " +
                          share.userName());

       share1.setUserName("Fred");                              //3
       System.out.println("User with shared access is " +
                          share.userName());
     }
   }
```

The output of this code is:

```
   User with shared access is Duke
   User with shared access is Fred
```

What went wrong? This code creates a `User` object, `share1`, at //1, with the user name `Duke`. A supposedly immutable `DiskDriveInfo` object is created at //2 and is passed a reference to the `User` object. The `DiskDriveInfo` object is queried and the shared owner, `Duke`, is printed. The `User` object, `share1`, changes its name to `Fred` at //3. When the `DiskDriveInfo` object is queried again for the user name, it discovers that the name changed from `Duke` to `Fred`.

217

The problem is that the DiskDriveInfo constructor receives a reference to the User object and does not make a copy, or clone, of this object. PRAXIS 1 explains that parameters are passed by value. Therefore, the DiskDriveInfo constructor receives a copy of the reference to the User object. Now the DiskDriveInfo object's driveShare field and the local variable, share1, in main of class Test, reference the same object. Therefore, any changes made through either reference affect the same object. The following diagram shows the object layout after the code at //1 is executed:

After the code at //2 is executed, the object layout looks like this:

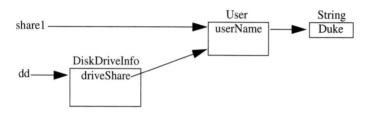

Notice that because the reference to the User object is not cloned, both the share1 and driveShare references share the same User object. After the code at //3 is executed, the object layout looks like this:

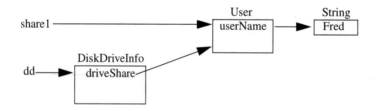

Shallow Cloning

To correct this problem, you can use a technique called *shallow cloning*. A shallow clone is a bitwise copy of an object. If the object being cloned contains object references, then the new object contains exact copies of the object references from the cloned object. Therefore, the new object and the cloned object still share data.

The DiskDriveInfo class must clone any mutable object to which it receives a reference. It then has a reference to its own copy of the object that cannot be changed by other code.

The modified DiskDriveInfo class that supports cloning looks like this:

```
final class DiskDriveInfo
{
  //As before...
  DiskDriveInfo(int size, String volLabel, User share)
  {
    driveSize = size;
    volumeLabel = volLabel;
    driveShare = (User)share.clone();
  }
  public User share()
  {
    return (User)driveShare.clone();
  }
}
```

Because you are cloning the User object, its definition must change as well. If you cannot change the User class to add the clone behavior, you must resort to other means. One solution is to modify the DiskDriveInfo class so it does not use the User object. Instead, the DiskDriveInfo class can store the String that represents the user name and the int that represents the user node.

Assuming that you have access to the User object, you must modify it to support cloning. To support a default, shallow clone, you need only to implement the Cloneable interface and to provide a clone method. (For more on cloning and why super.clone is called, see PRAXIS 66.) The modified User class looks like this:

```
class User implements Cloneable
{
  //As before...
  public Object clone()
  {
    try {
      return super.clone();
    }
    catch (CloneNotSupportedException e) {
      //This should not happen, since this class is Cloneable.
      throw new InternalError();
    }
  }
}
```

With these changes to the User object, running the previous test code produces the correct output:

```
User share1 = new User("Duke", 10);
DiskDriveInfo dd = new DiskDriveInfo(sizeInMeg, "myDrive",
                                     share1);
User share = dd.share();
System.out.println("User with shared access is " +
                   share.userName());

share1.setUserName("Fred");                                    //1
System.out.println("User with shared access is " +
                   share.userName());
```

This code produces:

```
User with shared access is Duke
User with shared access is Duke
```

Because the User object is cloned on the constructor call, the code that subsequently changes the User object at //1 has no effect on the DiskDriveInfo object. The implementation of the immutable DiskDriveInfo class is now correct. The object layout looks like this:

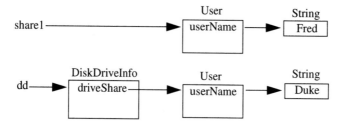

Returning a reference to a mutable object that is referred to in an immutable object presents the same problem. That is, code could gain access to your internal data and change it. Thus, you must clone any mutable objects for which a reference is returned.

For example, a reference to the User object, driveShare, is returned by the share method of the DiskDriveInfo class. The driveShare object needs to be cloned before it is returned from this method. It is not enough only to define a class without setter methods. You must be careful about how you receive and return object references.

You might wonder about the String and int parameters. They do not need to be cloned. Because the String class as well as all primitives are immutable, they cannot be changed by other code. Therefore, they do not present a problem.

Vector and Cloning

What happens if the implementation of the DiskDriveInfo class is changed to store a Vector of User objects that have shared access to the drive? Recall that the current implementation supports only one User object that has shared access. The DiskDriveInfo class now looks like this:

```
final class DiskDriveInfo
{
  //As before...
  private Vector driveShare;

  DiskDriveInfo(int size, String volLabel, Vector share)
  {
    //As before...
    driveShare = (Vector)share.clone();
  }
  //As before...
  public Vector share()
  {
    return (Vector)driveShare.clone();
  }
}
```

The test program is then modified to support the Vector. When this program is run, the results might be surprising. The modified test program looks like this:

```
import java.util.*;
class Test
{
  private static final int sizeInMeg = 200;
  public static void main(String args[])
  {
    User share1 = new User("Duke", 10);
    User share2 = new User("Duke2", 11);
    Vector shareVec = new Vector(2);
    shareVec.add(share1);  //Store 2 shared users in the vector.
    shareVec.add(share2);
    DiskDriveInfo dd = new DiskDriveInfo(sizeInMeg, "myDrive",
                                         shareVec);              //1
```

```
        Vector share = dd.share();
        System.out.println("Users with shared access are " +
                    ((User)(share.get(0))).userName() + ", " +
                    ((User)(share.get(1))).userName());

        share1.setUserName("Fred");
        System.out.println("Users with shared access are " +
                    ((User)(share.get(0))).userName() + ", " +
                    ((User)(share.get(1))).userName());
    }
}
```

This code produces the following output:

```
Users with shared access are Duke, Duke2
Users with shared access are Fred, Duke2
```

This is not the expected result. What happened? The only change made to this DiskDriveInfo class was to add a Vector to store multiple User objects that have shared access.

The problem is in the cloning of the Vector of User objects. By default, the clone method of the Vector class performs a shallow clone. The fields of a Vector are object references. Thus, in the previous code, when the Vector is cloned, a new copy of it is made. However, the contents of the Vector, which are object references, are not cloned. The following diagram shows the object layout after the code at //1 is executed:

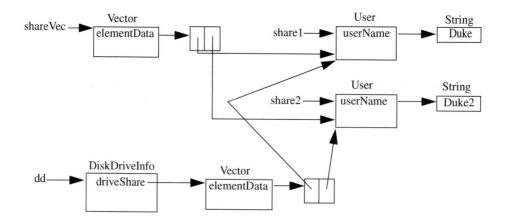

Deep Cloning

Because the default implementation of the clone method of the Vector class is a shallow clone, you must provide your own *deep clone* code. A deep clone ensures that the elementData field of the Vector in the DiskDriveInfo object refer- ences its own copies of the User objects instead of the User objects referenced by the shareVec variable. This ensures that the DiskDriveInfo object remains immutable.

One way to solve this problem is to subclass Vector, override its clone method, and provide your own implementation that performs a deep clone. The following code shows the deep clone implementation of the clone method of the subclassed Vector:

```
class ShareVector extends Vector
{
  ShareVector(int size)
  {
    super(size);
  }

  public Object clone()
  {
    ShareVector v = (ShareVector)super.clone();
    int size = size();                      //Create a new Vector.
    for (int i=0; i<size; i++)              //Replace each element
    {                                       //in the Vector with a
      User u = (User)(this.get(i));         //clone of that
      v.setElementAt((User)(u.clone()), i); //element.
    }
    return v;
  }
}
```

Notice that this code clones each object referenced by each element in the Vector. Changing the DiskDriveInfo class and the test code to use the ShareVector implementation produces the correct results. After the deep clone is performed, the object's representation looks like this:

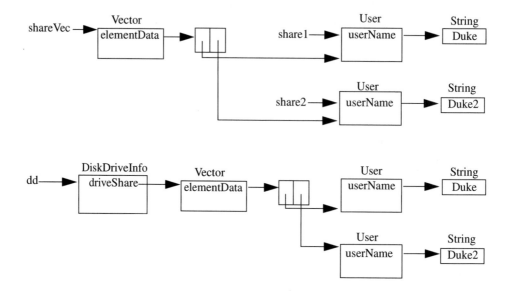

Now, changes made through the shareVec object reference will not affect the immutable DiskDriveInfo object.

This solution produces the desired results, but it has a few drawbacks. It requires the definition of a new class that is useful only to change the clone behavior of an existing class. In addition, it requires code that uses the DiskDriveInfo class to change. This code must now use the new ShareVector class instead of the Vector class.

An alternative solution is for the DiskDriveInfo class to individually clone the User objects itself. This is done in a private method to eliminate any code duplication. The modified DiskDriveInfo class looks like this:

```
final class DiskDriveInfo
{
  private int driveSize;
  private String volumeLabel;
  private Vector driveShare;

  DiskDriveInfo(int size, String volLabel, Vector share)
  {
    driveSize = size;
    volumeLabel = volLabel;
```

```
      driveShare = cloneVector(share);
    }
    public int size()
    {
      return driveSize;
    }
    public String label()
    {
      return volumeLabel;
    }
    public Vector share()
    {
      return cloneVector(driveShare);
    }
    private Vector cloneVector(Vector v)
    {
      int size = v.size();
      Vector newVector = new Vector(size);        //Create new Vector.
      for (int i=0; i<size; i++)                  //For each element
        newVector.add(((User)v.get(i)).clone());  //in the old Vector,
      return newVector;                           //add its clone to
    }                                             //the new Vector.
  }
```

This solution produces the desired results. It also has the added benefit that the code that uses the DiskDriveInfo class does not have to change.

In summary, follow these rules when implementing an immutable class:

- Declare the class final.

- Declare all data private.

- Provide only getter methods and no setter methods.

- Set all instance data in the constructor.

- Clone mutable objects for which a reference to them is returned.

- Clone mutable objects for which a reference to them is received.

- Implement a deep clone if the default shallow clone is not correct for a properly behaved immutable object. For more on cloning, see PRAXIS 66.

PRAXIS 65: Use inheritance or delegation to define immutable classes

PRAXIS 63 outlines some advantages of immutable objects and how to design and implement your own. This PRAXIS discusses three additional techniques that you can use to define immutable classes. Each has its own advantages and disadvantages. The techniques discussed are:

- Immutable interface

- Common interface or base class

- Immutable delegation class

Immutable interface

Assume you have an existing mutable class, MutableCircle, that represents a circle. Because of the thread-safety advantages of an immutable object, you want to let other code access an object of this class as an immutable object. The original MutableCircle class looks like this:

```
class MutableCircle
{
  private double radius;

  public MutableCircle(double r)
  {
    radius = r;
  }

  public void setRadius(double r)
  {
    radius = r;
  }

  public double radius()
  {
    return radius;
  }
  //...
}
```

To provide this class as an immutable class, you can declare an immutable inter-face that the mutable class implements. For example:

```
interface ImmutableCircle
{
  public double radius();
}

class MutableCircle implements ImmutableCircle
{
  private double radius;

  public MutableCircle(double r)
  {
    radius = r;
  }

  public void setRadius(double r)
  {
    radius = r;
  }

  public double radius()
  {
    return radius;
  }
  //...
}
```

Because the immutable `interface` exposes only the non-mutating methods of the underlying class, access to the object through the `interface` type preserves immutability. This allows you to use the immutable `interface` to prevent mutation. For example, the following code returns a reference to the `MutableCircle` object through the `ImmutableCircle` interface type, thereby properly preventing this code from compiling:

```
public class Test
{
  public ImmutableCircle createWheel(double r)
  {
    return new MutableCircle(r);
  }

  public static void main(String args[])
  {
    Test t = new Test();
    ImmutableCircle iWheel = t.createWheel(5.0);
    iWheel.setRadius(7.4);
  }
}
```

Note that the createWheel method returns a reference to an ImmutableCircle object. Objects of type ImmutableCircle can access only methods defined in the ImmutableCircle interface. In this case, the only method available is the non-mutating radius method. Attempts to access the methods of MutableCircle from an ImmutableCircle object reference are flagged by the compiler. Compiling the previous code results in the following error message:

```
Test.java:12: Method setRadius(double) not found in interface
ImmutableCircle.
    iWheel.setRadius(7.4);
                    ^
1 error
```

This is what you want to happen with code written in this way. This design, however, has a flaw. It works until the users of this class realize how to get around the immutability constraints you have established with the interface. Consider the following code, which breaks these immutability constraints:

```
public class Test
{
  public ImmutableCircle createWheel(double r)
  {
    return new MutableCircle(r);
  }

  public static void main(String args[])
  {
    Test t = new Test();
    ImmutableCircle iWheel = t.createWheel(5.0);
    System.out.println("Radius of wheel is " +
                       iWheel.radius());
    ((MutableCircle)iWheel).setRadius(7.4);
    System.out.println("Radius of wheel is now " +
                       iWheel.radius());
  }
}
```

This code not only compiles cleanly; it also generates the following output:

```
Radius of wheel is 5.0
Radius of wheel is now 7.4
```

The output shows that the supposedly immutable ImmutableCircle object has been altered. With this approach, however, users of the ImmutableCircle class can easily expunge its immutability with a simple cast. Remember, an interface declares a reference type. Therefore, an object reference of type ImmutableCircle can be cast to its derived type of `MutableCircle`. An object reference cast to a `MutableCircle` then can access the methods of this class and break immutability.

Because the programmer must extend the effort to code the cast, you might think this serves as enough of a deterrent. Nevertheless, the mutability constraints can be breached.

Common `interface` or Base Class

Preventing breaches of immutability requires another approach. One is to use one common `interface` or base class and two derived classes. These are organized as follows:

- An `interface` or `abstract` base class that contains the immutable methods that are common for its derived classes

- A derived class that provides a mutable implementation

- A derived class that provides an immutable implementation

For example, you might design an `interface` and two derived classes like this:

```
interface PinNumbers
{
  public String accountOwner();
  public int checkingPin();
  public int savingsPin();
}

class MutablePinNumbers implements PinNumbers
{
  private String acctOwner;
  private int checkingAcctPin;
  private int savingsAcctPin;

  MutablePinNumbers(String owner, int cPin, int sPin)
  {
    acctOwner = owner;
    checkingAcctPin = cPin;
    savingsAcctPin = sPin;
  }
  public void setAccountOwner(String str)
  {
    acctOwner = str;
  }
```

```java
    public String accountOwner()
    {
      return acctOwner;
    }
    public void setCheckingPin(int pin)
    {
      checkingAcctPin = pin;
    }
    public int checkingPin()
    {
      return checkingAcctPin;
    }
    public void setSavingsPin(int pin)
    {
      savingsAcctPin = pin;
    }
    public int savingsPin()
    {
      return savingsAcctPin;
    }
  }

  final class ImmutablePinNumbers implements PinNumbers
  {
    private String acctOwner;
    private int checkingAcctPin;
    private int savingsAcctPin;

    ImmutablePinNumbers(String owner, int cPin, int sPin)
    {
      acctOwner = owner;
      checkingAcctPin = cPin;
      savingsAcctPin = sPin;
    }
    public String accountOwner()
    {
      return acctOwner;
    }
    public int checkingPin()
    {
      return checkingAcctPin;
    }
    public int savingsPin()
    {
      return savingsAcctPin;
    }
  }
```

This technique allows a method to specify, in its signature,

- the mutable class, if it requires a mutable object,

- the immutable class, if it wants to preserve immutability, and

- the neutral `interface` or base class, if it does not care about immutability.

This solution also prevents the casting problem exposed with the immutable `interface` class. The immutability of these classes cannot be cast away. For example, consider the following code:

```
public void foo(MutablePinNumbers p)
{}
public void bar(ImmutablePinNumbers p)
{}
MutablePinNumbers m = new MutablePinNumbers("person1", 101,
                                            201);
ImmutablePinNumbers im = new ImmutablePinNumbers("person2", 102,
                                                 202);

foo((MutablePinNumbers)im);    //Compiler error
bar((ImmutablePinNumbers)m);   //Compiler error
```

Method `foo` takes an object reference of `MutablePinNumbers` as a parameter. Therefore, it can access the mutating methods of the `MutablePinNumbers` class. By contrast, method `bar` takes an object reference of type `ImmutablePinNumbers` as a parameter. Therefore, it cannot change the object referred to by parameter p. The object remains immutable for the duration of this method. If code tries to cast between these two types, the compiler generates an error.

This implementation ensures that the immutability constraints cannot be breached by a simple cast.

Immutable Delegation Class

Another approach uses an immutable delegation class. This class contains only immutable methods and delegates these calls to the mutable object it contains. For example, returning to the circle classes, the delegation technique looks like this:

```
class MutableCircle
{
  private double radius;
  public MutableCircle(double r)
  {
    radius = r;
  }

  public void setRadius(double r)
  {
    radius = r;
  }

  public double radius()
  {
    return radius;
  }
}

final class ImmutableCircle
{
  private MutableCircle mCircle;
  public ImmutableCircle(double r)
  {
    mCircle = new MutableCircle(r);
  }

  public double radius()
  {
    return mCircle.radius();
  }
}
```

The ImmutableCircle class uses layering, or the "has-a" relationship, with the MutableCircle class. When you create an ImmutableCircle object, you also create a MutableCircle object. Users of the ImmutableCircle object, however, cannot access the underlying MutableCircle object. They can access only the immutable methods provided in the ImmutableCircle class. Unlike the earlier immutable interface example, the user of these classes cannot cast between them.

This solution is particularly useful when you are unable to modify an existing mutable class. For example, the class might be part of a library you are using and you do not have access to the source code in order to use the other techniques. In this case, you can use the layering approach.

However, this solution has a downside. Coding the delegation model requires more work to implement and more effort to understand and maintain. In addition, a performance penalty is associated with each delegated method call. Consider these factors before deciding which technique to use.

The following table lists the advantages and disadvantages of the techniques to provide immutable objects.

Table 7: Immutability techniques

Technique	Advantages	Disadvantages
Immutable `interface`	Easy and straightforward. No performance penalty.	Can be breached.
Common `interface` or base class	Cannot be breached. Clean way to separate mutable objects from immutable objects.	Extra classes to implement. Deeper class hierarchy.
Immutable delegation class	Cannot be breached. Useful when you cannot change the source of an existing mutable class.	Performance penalty.

PRAXIS 66: **Call `super.clone` when implementing a `clone` method**

For classes that support cloning, the `clone` method of `java.lang.Object` must be invoked. This is accomplished by an implementation of a `clone` method invoking `super.clone`.

A `clone` method that begins with the `super.clone` invocation ensures that the `java.lang.Object` `clone` method is eventually called and the cloned object is constructed properly. This `clone` method creates a new object of the correct type and performs a shallow clone by copying all fields from the cloned object to the new object. However, even if you require a deep clone, you still need to invoke the `clone` method of `java.lang.Object` in order to create the correct type of object. (For a discussion of how a shallow clone and a deep clone differ, see PRAXIS 64.)

This `clone` method also ensures the correct derived object is created. Consider the following code:

```
class House implements Cloneable
{
  private int numberOfRooms;
  private int squareFeet;
  //...
  public Object clone()
  {
    return new House();
  }
}
```

For a class to support cloning, it must first implement the Cloneable interface. This interface is a marker interface, that is, it does not implement any methods. (For more on marker interfaces, see PRAXIS 59.) Classes that implement Cloneable advertise that they support cloning.

The implementation of the clone method in the previous class has a problem. It never calls super.clone. Consider what happens if the House class is subclassed and clone is called on the subclass:

```
class TwoStoryHouse extends House
{}

//...
TwoStoryHouse tsh = new TwoStoryHouse();
TwoStoryHouse other = (TwoStoryHouse)tsh.clone();  //Exception
//...
```

This code results in a runtime exception. The problem occurs when the clone method of the House class is called from a reference to a TwoStoryHouse. The clone method of House is invoked, and it creates an object of the class House and not of the class TwoStoryHouse. The following diagram shows the representation of the objects:

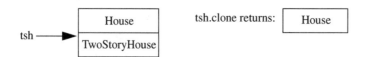

Therefore, the code attempts to cast an object of class House to a TwoStory-House. Because the object was not originally constructed as a TwoStoryHouse, a ClassCastException is thrown by the JVM at runtime.

This problem is fixed by properly implementing the clone method of the House class to call super.clone. Calling super.clone ensures that the clone method of java.lang.Object is called—this creates the correct type of object. A properly implemented clone method for the House class looks like this:

```
class House implements Cloneable
{
  //As before...
  public Object clone()
  {
    try {
      return super.clone();
    }
    catch (CloneNotSupportedException e) {
      throw new InternalError();
    }
  }
}
```

This implementation of the clone method guarantees that the clone method of java.lang.Object method is called. This ensures that the correct object is created so the code performing the cast does not fail. For example:

```
//...
TwoStoryHouse tsh = new TwoStoryHouse();
TwoStoryHouse other = (TwoStoryHouse)tsh.clone();  //OK
//...
```

The representations of the objects now look like this:

If you are implementing a deep clone, the same rule applies. You should call super.clone to acquire the correct type of object and then perform the deep cloning operations. This technique was implemented on the ShareVector class in PRAXIS 64.

PRAXIS 67: Do not rely on finalize methods for non-memory resource cleanup

The finalize method of a class is invoked by the JVM for an object of the class before the garbage collector reclaims its memory. This method is sometimes advertised as a way to ensure non-memory resources are freed before the memory for an object is reclaimed. Because the garbage collector frees only object memory, the `finalize` method provides a way to free other resources.

Programmers might place calls to close open sockets or file handles inside of a `finalize` method. The thinking is that this ensures that the program never runs out of these resources. In fact, the program can still run out of these resources regardless of the code in a `finalize` method.

The issue is that an object's `finalize` method is called before the garbage collector runs to free the storage for that object. PRAXIS 7 discusses that, depending on the garbage collection algorithm used, possibly not all eligible objects will be collected on a given execution of the garbage collector. In addition, `finalize` methods are not guaranteed to run at predictable times. This is because of the likely asynchronous nature of finalization and garbage collection. Consequently, the `finalize` methods of objects are not guaranteed to run before the program terminates. This means that even though you have coded the `finalize` methods properly to free non-memory resources, you can still deplete these resources before your program terminates.

One way potentially to avoid this problem is to use the `System.runFinalization` method. This method requests that the JVM invoke the `finalize` methods on all objects that have been identified as "finalizable" by a previous run of the garbage collector. Whether it does depends on the algorithms used in both the garbage collector and this method. However, there is no guarantee that invoking this method will run the `finalize` methods.

Another method previously available was the `System.runFinalizersOnExit` method, now deprecated. This method guaranteed only that the `finalize` method of all objects would run before the JVM exited. This meant that by the time the `finalize` method executed, you could already be out of resources. You typically want the `finalize` method to run during the execution of your program and not at the end when the JVM is exiting. This method was deemed unsafe and is deprecated in Java 2.

Therefore, you cannot rely on the `finalize` method for an object being called. You should implement your own non-memory resource cleanup mechanism that is used in conjunction with the class `finalize` method. You must ensure that classes that require such cleanup contain a `public` method that can be called to free the resources. This method should be called from the class `finalize` method to ensure that the non-memory resources are freed if the `finalize` method is invoked. If the `finalize` method is not invoked, the user can call the `public` method provided by the class as a way to free these resources. Consider the following class:

```
class Communication
{
  private ServerSocket ss;
  private FileInputStream fileIn;
  //...
  public synchronized void cleanup() throws IOException
  {
    if (ss != null)  //Check for null so we don't call close on an
    {                //already closed socket.
      ss.close();
      ss = null;
    }
    if (fileIn != null)  //Ditto
    {
      fileIn.close();
      fileIn = null;
    }
  }

  protected void finalize() throws Throwable
  {
    try {
      cleanup();
    }
    finally {
      super.finalize();  //Always call super.finalize in a finally
    }
  }
  //...
}
```

This class provides a `finalize` method that invokes the `cleanup` method. If the `finalize` method is called by the JVM, the non-memory resources are freed. Because the `cleanup` method is `public`, it also can be called by other code at any time. For example, you might implement a resource pool management framework that includes a `cleanup` method.

Depending on the design of your system, you should call the `cleanup` method of an object at regular intervals to ensure you do not run out of the resources the class manages. Because you might call it frequently, you must code it to handle multiple invocations properly. For example, notice that the `cleanup` method code is careful to check that the object references are not `null` before it calls their `close` methods. Furthermore, after the `close` methods are called, the object references are set to `null`. This ensures that multiple invocations of the `cleanup` method do not result in multiple calls to the `close` method. In addition, the `cleanup` method is declared `synchronized`. This guarantees that multiple threads do not enter this method concurrently for the same object.

The `finalize` method is also careful to call `super.finalize` from a `finally` block. (For more on `finally` blocks, see PRAXES 16, 21, and 22.) All `finalize` methods should call `super.finalize` to ensure that any superclass `finalize` methods are invoked. Unlike superclass constructors that are invoked automatically, `finalize` methods must be chained manually. The `super.finalize` call is made from a `finally` block to ensure that it is called regardless of whether the call to the `cleanup` method generates an exception.

Because you cannot guarantee if, or when, a `finalize` method is called, you should provide a `public` method to perform non-memory resource cleanup. This method should also be called by the class `finalize` method.

PRAXIS 68: Use care when calling non-final methods from constructors

A constructor for a class is invoked when a new instance of that class is created. The purpose of a constructor is to initialize an object. When the code in a constructor executes, it can call methods of its class. Constructors are often coded to do this because methods of the class might contain initialization code. For example:

```
class Base
{
  private int val;
  Base()
  {
    val = lookup();
  }

  public int lookup()
  {
    //Perform a database lookup
    int num = dbLookup();
    //return num;
    return 5;
  }
```

```
    public int value()
    {
      return val;
    }
}
```

The constructor for class Base calls a non-final method, lookup, to retrieve some data from a database. This code works as expected, with the instance data val, of class Base, being assigned the value 5. (Actually, the lookup method returns the value from the dbLookup method. The value 5 is returned for simplicity of illustration.)

Consider what happens if a derived class overrides the lookup method of class Base. Depending on how the overridden method is coded, this can lead to non-intuitive results. For example:

```
class Base
{
  private int val;
  Base()
  {
    val = lookup();
  }

  public int lookup()
  {
    //Perform a database lookup
    int num = dbLookup();
    //return num;
    return 5;
  }

  public int value()
  {
    return val;
  }
}

class Derived extends Base
{
  private int num = 10;
  public int lookup()
  {
    return num;
  }
}
```

```
class Test
{
  public static void main(String args[])
  {
    Derived d = new Derived();
    System.out.println("From main() d.value() returns " +
                        d.value());
  }
}
```

The output of this code is:

```
From main() d.value() returns 0
```

The problem is the method `lookup` of class `Derived` returned the value 0. You might wonder how this could happen, given the method's implementation. The method returns the value of the instance variable `num`, which is assigned the value 10 during instance variable initialization. However, instance variable initialization for class `Derived` has not occurred at the time its `lookup` method executes.

The `lookup` method is called from the constructor of class `Base` during the construction of an object of class `Derived`. When the `lookup` method of class `Derived` is entered, its instance variable initialization has not been performed. Its instance variables have only been set to their default initial values. In this case, `val` has been set to the value 0. Thus, 0 is returned from this method. (PRAXIS 32 analyzes the construction and initialization steps of objects in greater detail.)

This error can occur when a constructor calls a non-`final` method of its class. A problem results if this method is overridden by a derived class and that method returns a value that was initialized during instance variable initialization. This type of error might not be that common. However, knowing it exists can save a lot of time when you encounter it.

Appendix

Learning Java

> *A little learning is a dangerous thing.*
> —Alexander Pope

WHAT is the best way to learn and expand your knowledge of Java? I do not claim to know the best way, but I do know of a very effective way to enhance your Java development skills. I helped create a program at IBM that continues to be an effective learning tool.

Several years ago, I was asked to devise a way to mentor other programmers in IBM's lab on C++. At the time, I was involved in a fairly large C++ class library development project. I convinced three other C++ experts to join me, and we formulated a program called the "C++ Seminar Series." This series was so successful that we transformed it into the "Java Seminar Series" when our focus changed from C++ to Java.

The seminar series works as follows. Three or four people knowledgeable in Java, preferably experts, organize and run the group. These group leaders, or mentors, create a list of topics concerning Java that are of interest to learn. Each person who participates in the group must choose a topic from that list. Participants may also suggest their own topics, with mentor approval. The mentors then create a schedule of topics, their assigned presenters and dates for each participant's presentation. To give participants enough time to prepare a presentation, the mentors present for the first several weeks. This also helps set the tone and format for the remaining presentations.

Each participant researches the assigned topic and presents it to the rest of the group on the assigned day. We found that 90 minutes is enough time for each presentation. The group should meet on a regularly scheduled basis; in our experience, once a week works well and keeps the group moving. We also have a management sponsor who provides refreshments for each meeting. (This is, of course, an added bonus and does wonders for attendance.)

Group meetings should be as informal as possible and latitude should be given to participants regarding how they do their presentations. We do not require anyone to stand or use standard presentation charts. Whatever and however each participant thinks he or she can most effectively present the topic is allowed.

For some, it can be a little nerve-racking presenting a new topic to a group of people who might be unknown. To circumvent this problem, limit the attendance to only those who have signed up to do their own presentation. There is a certain comfort level in this. Each person knows that everyone else in the room is going to have his or her turn presenting.

The mentors are expected to know the presentation topic before the presentation. In this way, they can, during the presentations, help keep the discussion dynamic by asking relevant questions. The goal is not to embarrass anyone but to generate lively discussion and to encourage participants to learn as much as possible about the particular topic being presented.

It is also okay for a presenter not to know an answer to a question. Everyone knows that the presenter has had limited time to prepare for the topic and likely has not achieved expert status in that topic. In this case, the presenter notes the question and provides the answer in an e-mail message addressed to the rest of the group after the presentation.

If the presentation is in electronic format, it and any sample code are placed on a Web site that anyone can access. This Web site should also have other relevant information and links to Java resources.

Thus, the price for admission to the seminar series is to present a topic. The benefit is that participants learn from attending the other presentations, as well as from preparing their own. We require that each participant has at least a working knowledge of Java. We do not focus on introductory material, but rather on intermediate to advanced topics.

The number of people who join the group dictates how long that particular seminar series will run. In the past, we have had as few as 10 and as many as 40. With larger groups, however, the series can run too long. A good number is from 12 to

20. This results in a group small enough to be interactive, and the series ends in 15 to 25 weeks. (Assuming it meets once a week.)

Overall, this format has been very successful at IBM in Research Triangle Park, North Carolina. We ran two C++ seminar series a few years ago and most recently completed a second Java seminar series. Each time, as interest has spread, attendance has grown.

I encourage you to pilot a program such as this at your work location. It is a great opportunity for a group of people to learn more about Java. Furthermore, you have the opportunity to work with people from areas of your company whom you might not otherwise have the chance.

Further Reading

Everywhere I go I'm asked if I think the university
stifles writers. My opinion is that they don't stifle
enough of them.
—Flannery O'Connor

WHERE do you turn for definitive answers and information regarding Java and software engineering? A quick trip to the bookstore or your favorite Web site shows there is no shortage of Java books. The question is, which are worth having and provide the necessary information programmers need for developing with Java? The following list is by no means exhaustive. However, it contains the books and periodicals that I consult. I have read all of these, or at least representative portions of some, so that I can make a solid recommendation.

The Java™ Programming Language, Second Edition, Ken Arnold and James Gosling, Addison-Wesley, 1998, ISBN 0-201-31006-6.

This book is a good source for all of the language basics. In some cases it provides more expansive explanations of certain topics than does *The Java Language Specification*. Overall, it is an excellent tutorial with cogent discussion and clear examples.

The Java™ *Language Specification*, James Gosling, Bill Joy, and Guy Steele, Addison-Wesley, 1996, ISBN 0-201-63451-1.

For definitive information and answers on the Java language, look no further than this book. A *language lawyer's* dream, this book answers all questions relating to language specifics.

The Java™ *Virtual Machine Specification, Second Edition*, Tim Lindholm and Frank Yellin, Addison-Wesley, 1999, ISBN 0-201-43294-3.

For precise information about and answers regarding the details of a JVM, this is the book to own. To understand how a JVM is built, how it operates, how to port an existing JVM, or how to write your own, it is a must read. It also explains the JVM instruction set (the bytecodes) and is essential reading for compiler and JVM writers. Further, it provides detailed explanations about such topics as private and working memory of threads, object initialization, and synchronization.

As I wrote *Practical Java*, the preceding three books were never far from my reach. I consulted each continuously and thoroughly. I cannot imagine undertaking a serious Java development effort without them.

The Practice of Programming, Brian W. Kernighan and Rob Pike, Addison-Wesley, 1999, ISBN 0-201-61586-X.

This book, although not specifically about Java, provides language-independent advice and commentary on good programming practices. The authors bring decades of programming experience to a timely book that should be read by programmers working in any language.

Design Patterns: Elements of Reusable Object-Oriented Software, Erich Gamma, Richard Helm, Ralph Johnson, and John Vlissides, Addison-Wesley, 1995, ISBN 0-201-63361-2.

The bible of software patterns, this book should be read by all software designers and implementers.

Design Patterns CD: Elements of Reusable Object-Oriented Software, Erich Gamma, Richard Helm, Ralph Johnson, and John Vlissides, Addison-Wesley, 1998, ISBN 0-201-63498-8.

The CD-ROM version of the *Design Patterns* book.

Writing Efficient Programs, Jon Louis Bentley, Prentice Hall, 1982, ISBN 0-13-970251-2, or 0-13-970244-X (paperback).

Although this book is out of print, it is worth your time to find a copy. While the book is dated, and most of the code examples are in Pascal, the content is still relevant. Bentley provides solid advice and analysis of code efficiency.

Programming Pearls, *Second Edition*, Jon L. Bentley, Addison-Wesley, 2000, ISBN 0-201-65788-0.

This book is an excellent collection of essays on programming problems and their solutions. One section of the book is dedicated to performance.

Java Report, SIGS Publications, New York, NY.

This leading Java development magazine is well written and keeps getting better. It has wide coverage of all aspects of Java, from general industry-level information to detailed programming articles. Recently, the magazine has focused more on detailed programming articles about various aspects of Java development.

Index

When ideas fail, words come in very handy.
—Johann Wolfgang von Goethe

Note: The number in parenthesis following most of the page numbers is the PRAXIS number. Where it is missing, the entry concerns information outside of the PRAXIS text, such as preliminary chapter information.

249

C

Z

Colophon

The covers of this book are too far apart.
—Ambrose Bierce

Eᴌᴇᴄᴛʀᴏɴɪᴄ copy of this book was prepared by the author using Adobe FrameMaker 5.5.6 on an IBM Thinkpad 600E computer running Windows NT 4.0.

The text is primarily in Times, set 11 on 13. Section titles and quotations are also in Times at various sizes and weights. Pʀᴀxɪs titles are 12 point bold Times.

The font used for code is Lucida Sans Typewriter set at various sizes depending on where it is used. Code blocks are set 8.5 on 10.5, or 77 percent of the surrounding text. Elsewhere, code is 85 percent of the surrounding text.

The word, Pʀᴀxɪs, in Pʀᴀxɪs titles is in Lithos Regular with a point size of 14. Elsewhere, it is in Lithos Regular in varying sizes.

Don't let it end like this. Tell them I said something.
—last words of Pancho Villa